JOHN [SION] BARRINGTON was a hill shepherd, who lived in Rob Roy MacGregor's old house at the western end of Loch Katrine. He is a natural storyteller, a gift he exercises at schools, clubs and societies, and as an after dinner speaker. Stories are recounted on the move during daytime guided tours and twilight ghost walks. *Red Sky at Night* was his first book and won him a SAC Book Award. He now lives near Gartmore and does over 200 talks, tours and tastings every year – mostly within the Loch Lomond and The Trossachs National Park area.

Loch Lomond and The Trossachs

An A–Z of Loch Lomond and The Trossachs
National Park and surrounding area

To Mary Clare from
To Heather,
with love and every best wish.
John Barrington

JOHN BARRINGTON

Luath Press Limited
EDINBURGH
www.luath.co.uk

First published 2006

The paper used in this book is recyclable. It is made from
low-chlorine pulps produced in a low-energy, low-emission manner
from renewable forests.

Printed and bound by
Creative Print and Design, Ebbw Vale

Maps by Jim Lewis

All photographs by Danny Owens except Ellen's Isle by Ross Vernal

Typeset in 10.5 point Sabon

To M

Contents

G

H

I

J

CONTENTS

CONTENTS

Foreword

JOHN BARRINGTON – a shepherd and storyteller, a man with a passion for the natural and cultural heritage of Loch Lomond and the Trossachs. Who better to guide the reader on a tour through Scotland's First National Park and beyond? A tour with a difference. One that explores under the skin of the National Park to look at its history – fact and perhaps some romantic fiction. A story of the many generations of those who have lived and worked in the area; those who have helped shape the Park's special qualities, of which we are now so proud.

John Barrington must be described as a man of independent spirit. He and I do not always agree, and indeed there are statements made in his narrative with which I could not possibly concur. Nevertheless I respect his right to be controversial. John has never been one to keep his opinions to himself.

When the reconvened Scottish Parliament in one of its earliest acts put in place legislation to establish National Parks in Scotland, it set four aims for any Parks so designated, namely:

- to conserve and enhance the natural and cultural heritage of the area.
- to promote sustainable use of the natural resources of the area.
- to promote understanding and enjoyment (including enjoyment in the form of recreation) of the special qualities of the area by the public.
- to promote sustainable economic and social development of the area's communities.

The challenges have been set not only for our National Park Authorities but for all who are in the position to influence the future direction of our National Parks.

All of these aims are important but the real significance of an area such as Loch Lomond and the Trossachs National Park can only be recognised by further understanding of the special qualities which are there to be conserved and, dare I say, enhanced. An understanding of history, both natural and human, helps us all to appreciate the geography of what we are privileged to see in the Park today.

I applaud John Barrington's contribution to the goal of greater understanding, while stressing that there are no prizes for identifying sections of the narrative on which John and I beg to differ.

William Dalrymple
Chief Executive, Loch Lomond and The Trossachs National Park Authority
October 2006

Introduction

THIS BOOK BEGAN AS a newspaper series. *The Press and Post* was first published in February 2003, a direct attempt to provide the newly formed Loch Lomond and The Trossachs National Park with a firm sense of identity. The monthly journal has provided news and information both for the people who live and work within the Park and surrounding area, and for the huge numbers of visitors to this very special corner of Scotland.

I am indebted to James MacLean, editor of *The Press and Post*, for his encouragement and for publishing the articles. Also to Gavin MacDougall and his staff at Luath Press for making *Loch Lomond and The Trossachs* available in book form. Even though it has been thoroughly revised, I am well aware that some entries may soon be out of date – such is the vibrancy and speed of change in and around this young National Park. Under these circumstances a book can never be complete, so there is plenty of space at the end for your own notes and additions.

None of this would have been possible without the help and support of many people. First and foremost Marjory, my wife, who initially transcribed and electronically transmitted my badly hand-written copy, and then taught me to do it for myself! Thanks also to the helpful librarians at Drymen and Helensburgh, particularly to Mike Davis who was unstinting in his efforts on my behalf. Then there were the press officers who always returned my calls, especially those at Her Majesty's Naval Base, Faslane, and the National Park Authority's headquarters. Of the numerous others who provided me with so much valuable information, I am most grateful to John Mitchell of Drymen. And finally, the photographs taken by Danny Owens give a real flavour of this remarkable area.

John Barrington
Gartmore
October 2006

A

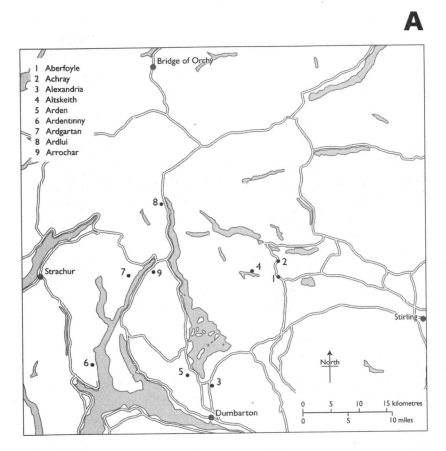

1 Aberfoyle
2 Achray
3 Alexandria
4 Altskeith
5 Arden
6 Ardentinny
7 Ardgartan
8 Ardlui
9 Arrochar

Bridge of Orchy

Strachur

Stirling

North

Dumbarton

0   5   10   15 kilometres

0   5   10 miles

Aberfoyle

Aberfoyle is rich in folklore and history, nestling on the southern edge of the Highland Boundary Fault. This is an area of spectacular mountains, lochs, rivers and forests. The Welsh sounding name is from the Brythonic language of the older Celts and means 'the confluence of the pool' from Brythonic *aber* – river mouth – and Scots Gaelic *phuill* – of a pool. This describes the place where the Duchray Water and the River Forth merge.

A claim to be 'the Enchanted Village' is certainly well founded. It was from the vicinity of his manse that, on 14 May 1692, the

Rev. Robert Kirk was carried away by the faeries. A learned man, Kirk had produced one of the first printed Gaelic Bibles. He also had a fascination and belief in the other world of the Little People. It was soon after the publication of his manuscript *The Secret Commonwealth of Elves, Fauns and Faeries*, in which he disclosed many of their secrets, that the minister disappeared.

Steeped in history, the imposing Inchrie Castle Hotel is built on the site of a battle fought between local Covenanters and government forces in 1693. More recently, in the spring of 1949, a conference at the hotel (whose name was changed recently from The Covenanters Inn) resulted in the writing of another covenant – pledging to ensure the return of a Scottish Parliament. Two million people were to sign this document. The so-called Stone of Destiny, probably an Edward I counterfeit, was hidden in the hotel after being liberated from Westminster Abbey on Christmas Eve 1950.

Aberfoyle has become a Mecca for walkers, cyclists, horse riders and teams of huskies who utilise almost 300 miles of forest trails. An interesting 18 hole golf course lies in the shadow of the Highlands. Aberfoyle is on the National Cycle Route 7 and the Rob Roy long-distance walk to Pitlochry. Little wonder then that the stained glass window in the Episcopal Church seems to depict an angel riding a bicycle – said to be the patron saint of tourism.

Achray

The name describes a flat, open place, in which the loch of the same name sits, reflecting the surrounding grandeur. However, most of the open spaces, whether flat or otherwise, have long been filled in by trees – the Achray Forest. The Forestry Commission has developed a spectacular seven mile forest drive, taking in three sparkling lochs. Many years ago, some illicit distillers only evaded the excise men by dumping the still and all their whisky into one of the lochs. The fish, of course, got very drunk – hence, Loch Drunkie.

The Achray Hotel, at one time a royal hunting lodge, has been greatly enlarged in recent years. A flock of tame sheep in the front field have eaten the daffodils marking the line of the old toll road, built by the Duke of Montrose in 1820. The tolls ended in 1931.

Long ago, iron was smelted in these Highland glens. Andrea Ferrara, the famous Venetian sword-smith, who had more smithies than Queen Elizabeth 1 of England, had beds worked here. An authenticated Ferrara sword came to light in the hotel – it has a small map showing the location of his local smithy clearly damascened on the blade.

It is an easy walk, a mile or so through the Trossachs, to Loch Katrine. Here is the setting of Sir Walter Scott's evocative poem, 'The Lady of the Lake', and the steamer bearing his name. The mini mountain of Ben A'an, not really a ben at all, is close at hand. The more challenging twin peaks of Ben Venue lie to the west. Wonderful views await those who make the summit. On a clear day, nine counties can be seen.

Alexandria

The town was named in 1760 after Alexander Smollett, local landowner, cotton manufacturer and Member of Parliament. It is one of the bleaching and manufacturing towns settled along the seven mile length of the River Leven, which meanders across just four miles between Loch Lomond and the Clyde. The present population stands at about 4,000.

Bleaching began in 1728 with the Dalquhurn Bleaching Company. Printing and dyeing of calico started in 1768. Industry diversified to include a car plant, a torpedo manufactury, a radium factory producing luminous paint, a tannery... and a whisky distillery. Opened in 1966, the Loch Lomond distillery is unique in producing both malt and grain whisky on the same site. The single malt has a blue label; the blend is sold with a red one.

Today Alexandria is known far and wide for the many craft and discount factory outlets. Eager shoppers flock by road and rail to snap up the latest bargains. The magnificent red sandstone Edwardian facade, built as the Argyll Car Plant, later to be used as a torpedo factory, now houses the Loch Lomond Shopping Centre. As a link to the past there is also a display of Scottish classic cars.

Sport has long been a feature of the Vale of Leven. The local football club, now a junior team, were founder members of the Scottish Football Association in 1873 and donated £1 towards a Scottish Cup. In 1877, the name 'Vale of Leven' was engraved onto the trophy after they defeated Glasgow Rangers 3–2.

There is a swimming pool in the town, an 18 hole golf course only a chip and a putt away, and Scotland's first National Park on the doorstep.

Altskeith

An ancient inn, now renowned as an excellent restaurant, on the shore of lovely Loch Ard, the Altskeith has simply the best view of Ben Lomond. The peaceful location belies the turbulent origin of the name. During a ferocious battle here in 711, between the local Britons and an army of invading Scots, the slaughter was so great that the small burn, flowing through the grounds, ran red far out into the loch – the stream spewing out blood.

In equally troubled times, Rob Roy MacGregor, very much a local boy, sought refuge in the building. The enemy were close on his heels. Rob was quickly hidden behind the wooden panelling of the parlour, the loose board concealed by a long-case clock. Once again the outlaw eluded the Redcoats who always seemed to be on his tail. On less pressing occasions, Rob would have enjoyed the convivial company and the hospitality of the Altskeith.

When the government tried to control distillation by a scheme of licences, nobody took much notice. Smith of Glenlivet was the first to apply, in 1824, but uptake was slow – after all, a licence did not make the whisky taste any better. Eventually most, including the Altskeith, came into line. Many were to lose their licence through some misdemeanour or other. The Altskeith, however, willingly relinquished their licence in 1860, in favour of buying in a number of choice whiskies. A fine selection is still available to the guests.

The Altskeith is ever popular with those who come for perfect peace. There are tree-shaded lawns and a pebble beach to laze on, quiet walks to enjoy and a couple of small rowing boats for hire.

Arden

Arden is probably derived from Gaelic *ard* – high, height or, in this case, a headland. Not much of the headland is left, having been greatly excavated. The sediment had been deposited by the Fruin as the water flowed into Loch Lomond. Now only flooded gravel pits remain, due to become features on a multi-million pound golf course development. This 284 acre (115 hectare) site has revealed some interesting archaeology.

A specified programme of investigation, agreed between the National Park Authority and the developers, has uncovered almost 4,000 years of history. Burial urns from three Bronze Age cemeteries have been dated back to c. 1800 BC. An entire Iron Age settlement was found which, amongst many other things, yielded up an extremely rare glass bead. An early Christian burial ground has been discovered. All very significant finds.

There are several magnificent houses at Arden. In the time of Robert Bruce, Auchendennan was a royal hunting estate. The present 19th century mansion became a youth hostel in 1924, and claimed to be the largest in the world. Lomond Castle, formerly Auchenheglish, has been redeveloped after a serious fire in 1990. Out of the ashes rose the Cruin restaurant, with wonderful views of the loch. Arden House was built by the Lord Provost of Glasgow in 1860. And then there is Bannachra Castle...

It was at Bannachra, in 1592, that Sir Humphrey Colquhoun was slain by a cuckolded husband – the chief of the MacFarlanes. When the secret of the affair got out, Colquhoun took refuge in Bannachra and MacFarlane laid siege. The end came when a treacherous servant illuminated his master as he passed an open window, presenting a perfect target to a waiting archer. Delicate bits of Sir Humphrey were served to his lover for breakfast!

Ardentinny

Over the hills to Ardentinny; a place much lauded in song. The great Sir Harry Lauder sang of it, as did Robert Tannahill. The name can be translated from Gaelic *Ard Teine* as the Height of the Beacon or Fire. With fine, open vistas down to the waters of the Clyde, Ardentinny could give valuable early warning of danger approaching from the sea. During the Viking period the beacon would have been lit on a fairly regular basis.

From the north, a narrow, tree-lined road, dominated by enclosing hills, runs the undulating length of Glen Finart. An alternative route, and a somewhat better road, skirts the shore of Loch Long. To the east of Ardentinny lie the much scarred hillsides of the Rosneath peninsular, and the Royal Navy Armaments Depot at Coulport. Large tankers also slip by to pump out their cargo of crude oil at the BP terminal at Finart.

Ardentinny is an excellent place for walkers. From the car park, to the north of the glen road, it is possible to simply stroll along the shore or wander through the adjacent woods. There are information boards giving details about the abundant wildlife of the area. The adventurous can hike all the way to Carrick Castle at Loch Goil, or even further.

A water sports centre caters for those who really enjoy getting wet. Others can just relax quietly on the shingle beach or take a little refreshment at the Ardentinny Hotel. There is a regular bus service from Dunoon Ferry Terminal, around the coastline, to Ardentinny and Glenfinart.

Ardgartan

Ardgartan, on the west side of Loch Long, guards the entrance to Glen Croe and the long haul up the A83 to the Rest and be Thankful. Here, more than anywhere in Scotland, earth meets sea meets sky. The land seems to flow right into the loch, while reaching up out of the trees to touch the heavens above. The sheer scale of the landscape is magnificent. Ardgartan means 'the Promontory of Thorn Bushes'.

This stretch of Loch Long, at Ardgartan, is extremely popular with divers. A comparatively safe area of deep, clear and sheltered water is known as Conger Alley. When diving, strict operational procedures must be observed. Extra oxygen should be available in case of emergencies. It will always take time to airlift a diving casualty to a Hyperbaric Chamber. (Sea anglers tend to stay safely out of the water.)

Overshadowed by the mighty Cobbler, the most distinctive of mountains, Ardgartan is just one of the starting points for the top. There are some sixty listed climbs to the triple summit, offering a full range of difficulty. Even though it misses the magical 3,000 ft, the Cobbler is the most popular mountain in Scotland. For the less adventurous, there are many miles of more gentle walks to enjoy from Ardgartan.

Part of the Argyll Forest Park, established in 1935, walkers, cyclists and horse riders can explore deep into the countryside. Close by will be deer, foxes, badgers, pine marten and wild cat. Many birds fly overhead, including the golden eagle. Just keep your eyes and ears open. Look out for rather strange wood-carvings lurking in the forest. Ardgartan is a perfect place for those who want to get away from everything.

Ardlui

Gaelic for 'Height of the Calves', this is an area where red deer hinds gather in May, ready to produce their young. Sheltered by the mountains, Ardlui is situated at the northern extremity of Loch Lomond. There is a shop, a hotel with a fine garden, a holiday home park, and a marina. Most visitors come by road or rail – Ardlui has a station on the West Highland Line. Others arrive by boat.

Weary walkers on the opposite shore, traipsing the West Highland Way, can hoist a signal to call the ferryman, bringing them back to civilisation. After a night of comfort they can return to the wilderness of east Loch Lomondside and go north to Fort William or south to Glasgow.

A little south of Ardlui there are two strange stone features.

Pulpit Rock is where ministers would conduct their services before the building of the kirk. While the sermon was preached to the front, refreshments were served round the back – well, they were rather long services! A vestibule has been cut into the rock; at one time it had a fine oak door.

Arrochar

Resting beneath the majestic Arrochar Alps at the head of Loch Long, Arrochar is a popular gathering place for hill climbers and mountaineers. This is Munro country – a land where many mountains reach up over 3,000 ft. Year round, the local population of 800 is enlarged by climbing enthusiasts from all over the world, who come to take on the challenging summits.

However, by far the most visited mountain is not a Munro. Ben Arthur, better known as the Cobbler, is only 2,899 ft/884 m. This prominent landmark of the old kingdom of Strathclyde may have a connection with the legendry Arthur. Its alternative name, the Cobbler, originally referred to the central peak and is a translation of *an greasaiche crom* – the crooked shoe maker.

Arrochar is derived from the Gaelic form of the Latin word *aratrum* – plough. The aratrum was an ancient Scottish square land measure of 104 acres/42 hectares. This was the area that could be ploughed by eight oxen in one year. *Loch* in Scottish Gaelic means lake of course; in Old Irish Gaelic it translates as dark. *Long* is a Norse word for ship. Loch Long is simply 'the Loch of the Ships'. It is also a long loch in the Modern English sense – 17 miles from end to end!

It was at Arrochar that, in 1263, the Vikings lifted a fleet of longboats out of the sea, carrying them overland to Loch Lomond. The consequences were devastating. Loch Long was later the testing area for torpedoes manufactured at Alexandria. There are no Vikings, no torpedoes and no droves of cattle passing through Arrochar today. The peace is only disturbed by the busy traffic moving between Central Scotland and Cowal.

B

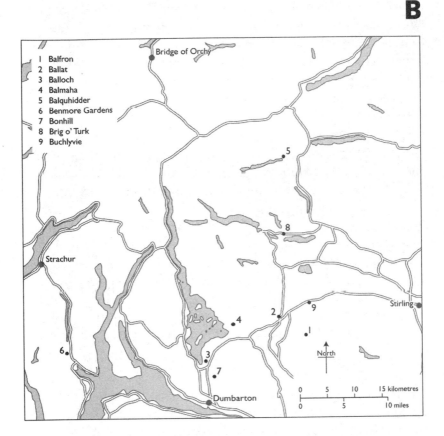

1 Balfron
2 Ballat
3 Balloch
4 Balmaha
5 Balquhidder
6 Benmore Gardens
7 Bonhill
8 Brig o' Turk
9 Buchlyvie

Bridge of Orchy

Strachur

Stirling

North

Dumbarton

0   5   10   15 kilometres
0   5   10 miles

Balfron

The first documentary appearance of Balfron is found in a charter dated 3 October 1303. This granted the titles of Buthbren (Balfron) to Inchaffray Abbey. The name comes from a very sad episode of the history of the village. A raid of wolves is said to have swept through the settlement, carrying off all the children. From then the place was known as Bail-a-bhroin – the town of mourning. (These 'wolves' were in reality Vikings.)

This quiet hamlet became swept up in the Industrial Revolution. Within the space of a couple of years, the population rose from 50 or so to 980. The original clachan clustered around the church expanded into a well-planned development, flowing down the hill to the cotton works on the banks of the Endrick Water. But the new natives soon became restless. Religious upheaval and political insurrection loomed.

Many of the Balfron weavers were involved in the 1820 uprising. A dozen Balfron radicals were amongst those put on trial at Stirling for treason. Two ringleaders, John Baird and Andrew Hardie, were beheaded on 8 September, the last in Britain to suffer this fate. The gruesome duty was carried out by a medical student from Glasgow, and the axe that he used and the gown that he wore are both on display at Stirling Museum. Most of the other rioters were released.

With the coming of the Forth and Clyde Railway, Balfron became a popular tourist resort. The trains have long stopped running but visitors still arrive by car and by bus. The views along the Endrick Valley from the village bowling green, and the panorama from the golf course, make a day trip to Balfron well worthwhile.

Ballat

Ballat is a major crossroad at the edge of Scotland's first National Park. Glasgow is to the south, Stirling to the east, and the roads north and west go directly into the park. Long ago, a fine freshwater spring refreshed passing animals and travellers, setting them up to continue their journey. Now a popular restaurant and filling station serve exactly the same needs.

Down the centuries, local women would gather around this spring to laboriously hand-wash their clothes, telling each other outrageous stories and singing sassy songs – it was a 'Place of Good Cheer'. This is precisely the meaning of the Gaelic name *Bail'ait*. Ballat is a natural watershed between the River Forth and the Endrick Water. The Bog of Ballat is an ancient hay meadow, renowned for interesting plants and rare insects.

It is not only traffic that hurtles through Ballat day and night. Every 24 hours, 100 million gallons of water (500 million litres) flow silently through Ballat, en route for Glasgow. Since 1859, Loch Katrine has been the main reservoir for Scotland's largest city. A substantial stone bridge carries the water over the busy A81. Some of the houses in Ballat were built for Water Board workers.

At the Spittal of Ballat, formerly a small farm, Knights Hospitallers would have tended the needs and requirements of many travellers. The Knights Templars who survived the mass assassination attempt orchestrated by the Pope and Philip IV, fled to Scotland. The onslaught took place on Friday 13 October 1307, which is why Friday the Thirteenth is now deemed to be unlucky, especially if you happen to be a Knight Templar.

Balloch

Balloch, from the Gaelic *bealach*, means a gap or a pass. This is the pass through which the Great West Road (A82) leads into the Highlands and to the islands of the west. In days when travel and transport were largely by water, Balloch was strategically placed at the southern end of Loch Lomond, the greatest sheet of water in Britain. Here the River Leven gave egress to the Clyde and the whole world beyond.

First road and then rail links followed, the Balloch ford became a bridge, and Balloch prospered. Cattle droves that were prepared to pay the tolls passed through the town on their way to the trysts of Dumbarton, Muir and Falkirk. The rest simply swam the loch higher up. Produce from the Highlands and fish from the loch were required to feed the textile workers of the Vale in ever increasing amounts.

Glaswegians poured out of town to escape the industrial grime and breathe in fresh air. Visitors from further afield soon began to discover the delights of the bonnie banks of Loch Lomond. Finally, after many years of discussion, Scotland's first National Park became a reality. In 2000 the new authority set up camp in a collection of portacabins. However, an imposing visitor centre, with a cluster of shops and an excellent information and education complex, has become the fulcrum of the park.

In the shadow of Drumkinnon Tower, a 50 year old paddle steamer sits at her mooring. The *Maid of the Loch* was the last of her kind to be built in Britain. Undergoing a complete refit, she is already operating as a restaurant and function venue. When the work is finished, it is hoped to have the *Maid of the Loch* plying the waters once more.

Balmaha

Balmaha is a busy staging post and important watering hole for walkers on the West Highland Way. It is also the terminus for the buses from Alexandria and Balloch. The modern pronunciation of Balmaha suggests *Baile mo Thatha* – the Township of St Maha. But *baile*, shortened to *bal*, does not appear in place names before the 12th century. As St Maha was a 5th century companion of St Patrick, the correct spelling is likely to be *Buaile mo Thatha* – the Fold or Enclosure of St Maha.

Balmaha is an absolute haven for small boats. From the wooden jetty at the boat yard, it is possible to sail out on the morning mailboat run – daily in high summer, less frequently at other times. Three of the islands are permanently inhabited. You can also be ferried to one of the other islands and left for a while. There is much to explore.

The closest island is Inchcailloch – the Island of the Nuns. This is one of a chain clearly marking the line of the Highland Boundary Fault. The holy women are long gone, although their chapel was in regular use until 1670. The last funeral took place in 1947. When Gregor, chief of Clan Gregor, was laid to rest in 1692, the pipers composed a tune for the occasion – 'Hail to the Chief'. This has become the anthem of American Presidents.

The wildlife at Balmaha, where Highlands and Lowlands meet, is extensive and rather surprising. Unique lamphrey, rare powan and huge pike live in the loch. Osprey hunt overhead, waiting to snatch a salmon or trout from the water. Deer, foxes, badgers and wildcats lurk in the forest. And watch out for the Balmaha Bears! They feature in a series of imaginative stories, published by Glow-worm Books.

Balquhidder

This typical long, straggling glen has, from time immemorial, been associated with cattle farming. Balquhidder seems to come from *Baile Foidir* – *baile* is Gaelic for settlement; *foidir* is the Gaelic version of the Old Norse word *fothr*, meaning fodder. The narrow, loch-filled glen is sheltered, fertile and secure. People have long been settled on its braes, leaving stone carved cup and ring marks from earliest times.

Balquhidder stretches from Beinn Chabhair, in the west, to Balquhidder Station on the A84. The village is tucked just inside the mouth of the glen, guarded at the entrance by the Kingshouse. This inn, built in 1571, was commissioned as accommodation for road-building soldiers in 1779. All traffic entering and leaving the glen passes right by the door of the Kingshouse Hotel.

Long ago, these were MacLaren lands. In troubled times their clansmen would rally at *Creag an Tuirc* – 'the Rock of the Boar', a high point overlooking the church. Later, a few MacGregors moved in as neighbours, causing a little bit of friction! Rob Roy MacGregor is buried in Balquhidder. He died peacefully in his bed at the age of 74 – not a bad end for the old outlaw.

St Angus brought Christianity to Balquhidder in the 6th century. At the point where he first saw into this beautiful glen, Angus knelt to give thanks. On that spot is a house, still known as 'the Blessings of Angus'. The present church was built in 1853, and is the third kirk on the site. If you need a reason to visit, come to one of the summer Sunday evening concerts, held in the church – then you could dine either at the Kingshouse or at the heart of the glen, at the splendid Monachyle Mhor.

Benmore Gardens

The Younger Botanic Gardens are almost 200 years old and famous for a magnificent collection of trees and shrubs. Situated in the well-sheltered Glen Eachaig, between Loch Eck and the Holy Loch, the plants flourish in an equitable climate. The 140 acre (57 hectare) garden is set in natural woodland and overlooked by imposing hills, including the impressive Beinn Mhor (2434 ft/742 m) to the north.

The Royal Botanic Gardens, established in 1670, acquired Benmore in the last century, turning it into one of their specialist gardens. At the entrance is a spectacular avenue of giant redwoods, planted in 1863 and now over 130 ft/40 m high. Throughout the gardens are way-marked walks, which lead to a beautiful pond and to a formal garden with a wide variety of Himalayan plants.

Stroll through the Glen Massan Arboretum and admire some of the tallest trees in Scotland. One Douglas fir measures 180 ft/55 m. The richly planted slopes of Benmore Hill offer splendid views of the Eachaig valley and down to the Holy Loch, with the Firth of Clyde beyond. Over 250 species of rhododendron put on a great floral show. Many are just as interesting for their foliage and textured bark.

The gardens are open every day, with a free car park and good disabled facilities. The James Duncan Café, named for the sugar baron who built Benmore House, serves delicious food and is fully licensed. A shop sells a range of gifts, books, local crafts and plants. At Benmore there is something for everyone, a wealth of year-round interest. The wild Cowal scenery will make the journey to Benmore really worthwhile.

Bonhill

Bonhill would have been the first fording point across the River Leven, below Balloch. The name comes from the Gaelic *Bun Uill* – Village at the Foot of the Burn. The burn itself has long been piped underground, and runs quietly beneath Burn Street before emptying into the river. A fine metal bridge now spans the Leven, linking the community with Alexandria.

The square towered church, more securely locked than Fort Knox, stands on a much older site. There has been a place of worship here since the late 12th century. Amongst the graves is that of Robert Nairn, cobbler and Covenanter – and very active in the cause. Nairn was eventually buried, under great duress, by the Episcopal minister of the day. It would seem that the cobbler had very persuasive friends.

Bonhill primary school dates from 1873 but was not the only place of learning. During the Industrial Revolution, which brought the cotton mills to the Vale, some employers had enlightened views. They would ensure that their child workers were provided with a proper education, paid for by the company. It may not have been much, but it was a start.

There is plenty of scope for recreation. Bonhill has Loch Lomond and the National Park right on its doorstep. Walks to the east take in Pappert Hill and Auchenreoch Muir, a strange world of cairns and standing stones. And there is sport: a nine hole golf course, football and rugby. The newly promoted Loch Lomond Rugby Club plays at Bonhill and hopes to continue up through the league in the coming seasons.

Brig o' Turk

This is 'the Bridge of the Boar', stone built in 1796 and widened in 1929. There are accounts of much earlier wooden structures, going right back to 1451. The tracks using these ancient bridges were probably quite poor, but not as bad as the roads of today. With crumbling edges and deep potholes, the roads around Brig o' Turk have become unsafe. So much so, the locals have taken to putting up notices to warn of the dangers.

The first school opened in 1719 and the present building dates from 1875. The beautiful church of St Kessog is at a little distance, on the shore of Loch Achray. Designed by G.P. Kennedy, one of the architects of the Westminster Parliament, couples come from all around the world to be married in the Trossachs. The setting is absolutely magnificent.

There are many walks from Brig o' Turk. The most popular route is north, a quiet road leading to the newly created loch in Glen Finglas. From here it is possible to go through the hills to Balquhidder, or take a lengthy loop around Meall Cala (14.5 miles). After a hard day's tramping, refreshments are available at the Byre Inn and the quaint tearoom, which is also a licensed restaurant. The Brig o' Turk Tearoom opened in 1923 and featured in the film, *The Thirty-nine Steps*, starring Kenneth More. Fame indeed!

Near the tearoom, on the site of an old smithy, stands a strange, iron-eating sycamore tree. If you look carefully, you will see partially digested bits of rusty metal, including an anchor on a chain and a bicycle.

There is a daily postbus to Brig o' Turk and, in the summer, the Trossachs Trundler does just what its name implies several times a day – linking with Aberfoyle and Callander.

Buchlyvie

Buchlyvie may commemorate a long forgotten battle in the name *Buaidh Chaidheamh*, proclaiming 'the Victory of the Sword'. Through the years the spelling has varied – Bucklyvie, Bollchlyvie, and even Ballchlavie. The exact origins are shrouded in the grey mists of time. What is clear, however, is that these lands were held by the Marquis of Montrose in the second half of the 17th century.

The village is said to have been founded by Sir Andrew Graham, the second son of Montrose, in 1680. Sir Walter Scott referred to Andrew Graham as the Baron of Buchlyvie. A much more famous Baron of Buchlyvie was a horse – a Clydesdale stallion whose skeleton is kept in the Glasgow Art Gallery. He would cover 400 mares each season, at £60 a time, with another £60 to be paid if a foal was produced. In 1904, the Baron's leg was shattered by a vexatious female. Such is life.

Buchlyvie was the setting for one of Rob Roy MacGregor's exploits, a cattle raid known as the Hership of Kippen. Rob had planned to intercept a large drove belonging to the anti-Jacobite, Sir Alexander Livingstone. Before the cattle appeared, the drovers, with help from Balfron and Kippen, tried to repel the Highlanders. As a reprisal for this intrusion, MacGregor not only seized Livingstone's herd, but also emptied Kippen's fields.

Buchlyvie is very much a place you pass through. If you do make time to stop for a while, there are two inns, a tearoom, a pottery shop and, at the bottom of the village, a farm shop that is well worth a visit.

C

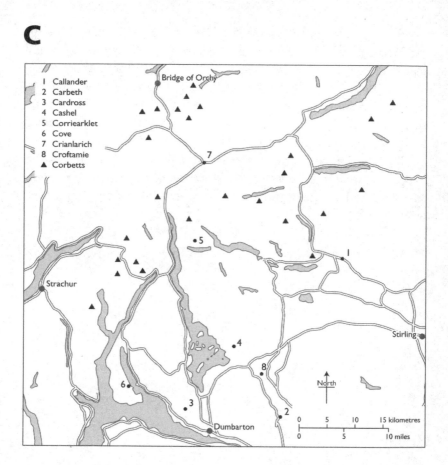

1 Callander
2 Carbeth
3 Cardross
4 Cashel
5 Corriearklet
6 Cove
7 Crianlarich
8 Croftamie
▲ Corbetts

Bridge of Orchy

7

Strachur

5

1

Stirling

4

8

North

6

3

2

Dumbarton

0   5   10   15 kilometres
0   5   10 miles

Callander

Mentioned as Calentare in 1164 and Callanter in 1350, Callander translates from Gaelic *Call Dobhar* as 'Hazel Water' or *Caled Dobhar* as 'Rough Water'. This well known tourist centre stands on the River Teith, formed by the confluence of Garbh Uisge and Eas Gobhain. To the north of the town, the bulwark of the Highlands dominates the skyline, Ben Ledi (2,883 ft/879 m) is head and shoulders above the rest.

The road north from Callander, leading through the Pass of Leny, has been greatly improved. This is one of only four entries into the Scottish Highlands – a very busy route. The ancient Chapel of St Bride, nestling inside the pass, has been partially restored as a memorial to Sir Walter Scott, a frequent visitor. J.M. Barrie had associations with the 17th century Roman Camp Hotel here, renowned for its cuisine.

The Romans, when they were here, camped to the north of the site of the town – a blockade on the Highland exit. A ghostly cohort is sometimes heard marching through the night, orders still being shouted in Latin. Tourists through the ages have enjoyed the delights of Callander. An example of early town planning, Callander predates Edinburgh's New Town by some 10 years.

The striking Gothic church of St Kessog, built in 1883, is now the Rob Roy Visitor Centre. The wonderful sights that delight our visitors were all well known to Rob Roy. There is a steep walk up Callander Crags, eventually leading to the spectacular Bracklinn Falls. To the west lie beautiful Loch Vennachar and the ever-enchanting Trossachs.

Carbeth

Carbeth sits on the A809, a quiet and scenic road from Glasgow to the National Park and the south end of Loch Lomond. The name is a reference to a vanished stronghold, meaning 'the Fort Amongst the Birches'. The most prominent feature is the low, neat, whitewashed inn at the roadside. Halfway from Dumbarton to Stirling, halfway between Drymen and Glasgow, Carbeth is ideally placed.

Here the Highland cattle drovers would rest and water their charges – and themselves, mingling with the merchants, travellers and the odd smuggler. The tradition of a warm welcome and excellent food continues. The clientele may have changed; the service is just the same. This is hospitality at its best, earning Carbeth Inn a deserved entry in *Scotland Recommended 2003*.

The Carbeth Trout Fishery has both fly and bait ponds. Rod and net hire is available and there is good disabled access. The ponds are stocked daily, the fine rainbow trout weighing up to 20 lb (9 kg).

There are plenty of birds to watch while waiting for a bite. For walkers, it is a short step to the Queen's View, where Queen Victoria stood looking into her Highlands. There are challenging climbs at the Whangie and at Creagmore.

The hill behind Carbeth is speckled with huts, originally little holiday refuges from the heavy grime of industrial Glasgow. The old city has certainly cleaned up its act, but new generations of hutters continue to bring life and colour to the area, enjoying all Carbeth has to offer.

At one time served by stagecoach, there is a bus service from Balfron, via Drymen, to Glasgow.

Cardross

It was at Cardross that Robert Bruce, Liberator of Scotland, spent his last days. He died from leprosy, in his manor house on the banks of the Leven, on 7 June 1329. But there is more to Cardross than the end of an ailing king, much more. To protect the exposed western flank of the Antonine Wall, the Romans had a fort on Ardmore Point; the landing place in White Bay can still be seen. This was the last outpost of the Empire, with wild Caledonia beyond. Cardross can be translated as 'the Fort on the Promontory'.

In the 5th century, St Maha superimposed a church on a Celtic pagan site. A new church was consecrated in 1467 by the Bishop of Argyll – this was in the parish of Rosneath. Restored again in 1953, the little Chapel of St Mahew is still in use. A larger, Protestant church was built on a different site in 1644, redeveloped in 1826, and blitzed in 1941. The shell still stands, with an interesting pair of carved faces at the south door.

Kilmahew Castle was held by the Napiers from the 13th to the 19th centuries. These lands were granted to Duncan for services to Malcolm, Celtic Earl of Lennox. A six hole golf course opened at Kilmahew in 1895, and a new 18 hole course in 1904. The clubhouse also perished in the 1941 bombing; new premises were ready for business in 1956. Cardross has produced two Amateur and one Professional Scottish Golf Champions.

Cardross was a busy place, with mills on several burns and a tile works making use of the local clay. The railway arrived in 1858 – and is still going strong. There used to be two ferries crossing the Clyde to Port Glasgow. The Erskine Toll Bridge is probably as expensive, but much more convenient.

Cashel

Cashel is the English rendition of *caiseal*, a castle. The change in pronunciation from s to sh is common in Gaelic. There are many brochs, castles, duns and forts in this part of Scotland, with its turbulent history. This particular castle, on Strathcashell Point, protected on three sides by the waters of Loch Lomond, is said to have been one of the strongholds of Finn McCoul.

Cashel Farm is part of the National Memorial Park, bought by public money – twice! It was first purchased after World War II by money raised through the sale of army surplus, as a lasting tribute to all who died for their country. But memories fade, even official ones, and Cashel was inadvertently sold to the tenant farmer. This caused a bit of a rumpus but, when the dust had settled, Cashel was bought back for the nation.

The livestock having left with the farmer, Cashel is being returned to native woodland. It is hoped that Cashel will soon look like it did in ages past, before the coming of the sheep. The land is being managed by the Royal Scottish Forestry Society Trust, and the aim is to eventually restore a 3,000 acre (1,214 hectare) forest. The planting of Scots pine and native broadleaved trees is well under way.

Individuals and communities are encouraged to become involved with the scheme. Several local schools are engaged in projects on the site, building shielings, digging lazybeds, spinning wool, getting a real feel of the lives of their ancestors. There are many fine walks to enjoy, all graded and waymarked. The green route, a circular 4 mile (6.5 km) walk, has almost 1,000 ft ascent. This will give great views over Loch Lomond and the forest being created for the next thousand years.

Corbetts

Within the boundary of the Loch Lomond and Trossachs National Park, there are 20 mountains between 2,500 ft and 2,999 ft, with another 13 within easy distance. That is a good percentage of the 221 Scottish mountains classified as Corbetts. Combined with the 21 Munros inside the park (with 10 more close at hand), there is a lot of climbing to be had.

John Rooke Corbett was a keen member of the Scottish Mountaineering Club, and completed his Munro list in 1930. Having done so he set about everything over 2,000 ft, though the list was not published until after his death. Corbett insisted on a descent of 500 ft on all sides of a summit, making his mountains more clearly defined than Munros.

Some may consider Corbetts to be rather inferior hills – they most certainly are not. With the likes of the Cobbler (2,899 ft/884 m), Beinn a'Choin (2,525 ft/770 m) and Beinn Odhar (2,995 ft/901 m) in the area, climbers are spoiled for choice. These are some of the finest hills in Scotland. Whatever they lack in height they more than make up for in character. And the views are just as good!

In Scotland there has always been a freedom to roam on the hills and moorland, now enshrined in law. With these rights come a few responsibilities: to take care of our countryside and remember that some people make their living from these hills. At certain times of the year there will be lambing, grouse shooting and deer stalking. Also take care of yourself. Be sure to be properly kitted out, and that someone knows where you are going.

Corriearklet

Until recently, Corriearklet was part of the largest sheep farm in Britain, stretching from Loch Arklet to Beinn A'an, at the east end of Loch Katrine. The landowners, Scottish Water, went into the new millennium determined to remove the sheep, the cattle having already been sold. The people soon followed, drifting out of the glens – a new Highland Clearance had arrived.

The name is derived from Gaelic *coire* – a corrie or mountain hollow – *airc* – steep or difficult – and *leathad* – a slope. There are steep slopes all around, across Loch Arklet and either side of the Corriearklet Glen. The views keep changing with the light, reflecting from the water, reflected off the hillsides. Away to the west, beyond Loch Lomond, the Arrochar Alps never look the same way twice.

It was at Corriearklet that Rob Roy MacGregor married Mary of Comer, on New Year's Day 1693. This is also the site of a terrible battle between the Scots from Argyll and the local Britons. The Scots won the battle but not the war. The Brythonic language (ancestor of modern Welsh) was spoken here until 1400. Queen Victoria stopped at Corriearklet during her visit to Inversnaid, on 2 October 1869. Quite a history for a small place.

Gerard Manley Hopkins, a gentle Jesuit priest, was a frequent visitor to Corriearklet. He would walk in the glen, seeking solitude and communing with the nature all around. Many of his observations have been recorded in his wonderful poetry – never intended for publication. Even without the blackface sheep, there is plenty to gladden the eye.

There is a small parking area about 300 ft towards the west. The roads are narrow, so please do not park in passing places.

Cove

Cove, on Loch Long, does not take its name from the bay it undoubtedly is, but from the Old Norse word *kofi* – a hut. Facing west, Cove has sweeping, breathtaking views across the loch and right down the Firth of Clyde. It is believed that either the Danes or Norwegians had a lookout tower at Cove. The ancient dungeons were supposedly incorporated into the building of Knockderry Castle in 1855.

The present buildings of Cove can hardly be described as huts. These are mostly the magnificent mansions of the industrial barons from Glasgow... and a few of the aristocracy. The stately pile of Lord Inverclyde is no more; an ultra modern fire station stands on the site. Cove is obviously a safety conscious place, housing a coastguard station with an inshore lifeboat – pretty essential in these busy waters.

About ten per cent of the population of the Rosneath peninsular, also called the Isle or Yl of Rosneath, are members of the Sailing Club. In front of the clubhouse is a new jetty, with a slipway into the loch, built with some lottery funding. Cove, along with Gourock and Aldeburgh in Suffolk, is one of the last places to sail and race Loch Long Keelboats. Designed and built in the area, they are well able to withstand the rigours of the Clyde.

The Linn Botanic Gardens are open all year, dawn till dusk. Linn relates to the wet ground below the rock face, flooded by the Meikle and Bogle Burns. The last quarter of the 20th century saw redevelopment and extension of the garden, which is best enjoyed from the network of paths. There will be some steep climbing to do, but it is well worth the effort.

There is a regular bus service from Helensburgh, going through to Coulport.

Crianlarich

Crianlarich means either 'A Little Pass' (*Crion Lairig*), which it is certainly not, or 'Aspen Trees by a Ruin' (*Critheann Laraich*). The latter is a more plausible derivation. Aspen was held in high regard by our ancestors. The wreaths or chaplets worn by the heroes of old would allow them to enter the mysterious Underworld and return quite unharmed. Shields made from aspen wood offered protection against supernatural forces as well as more mundane mortal powers.

Crianlarich is one of the last romantic railway junctions. Here the West Highland Line from Glasgow splits either side of Strath Fillan, to Oban and Fort William. At the junction trains are joined or divided and goods traffic, mostly timber, is shunted. Sixty miles from Queen Street Station, the final five miles into Crianlarich requires some serious climbing. This is waterfall country and the ascent is over 500 ft.

This is the heart of the ancient Celtic earldom of Breadalbane – the High Country of the Scots. Crianlarich is surrounded by the grandest and wildest mountain scenery in the National Park. It is rich, too, in folklore and legend, as tales of mythical warriors intertwine with stories of medieval saints. Perhaps a few of the old, gnarled pine trees, standing alongside the railway and the A82, witnessed such times.

Crianlarich is popular with walkers. The West Highland Way has given a boost to the local economy, and this is one of the favourite overnight halts. It has been claimed that it would be possible to fish a new river-beat or fresh loch every day for a year in this area – a challenge for any angler! But it is to the hills that many are drawn, for shooting, for stalking and, most of all, for climbing. Just as well Crianlarich is home to the Mountain Rescue Service.

Croftamie

This is 'Jamie's Croft'. Croft is a Middle English term for an enclosed piece of ground; later it came to mean 'a field with a dwelling'. It is a tiny village, today with 527 souls. Croftamie blossomed with the coming of the railway, becoming the station for nearby Drymen. The Duke of Montrose would not let the noisy, smelly, dirty trains anywhere near his domain at Buchanan Castle.

The Steam Age brought industry in its wake. Early motorcars were hand crafted and an innovative engine was designed and developed at Croftamie. Neither went into production, but there is one to be seen at the Museum of Transport, Glasgow. The railway closed, followed by an economic downturn, but Croftamie was resilient. A small industrial park occupies the old station site.

This is the place to come if you are looking for a new stove. The Scottish Stove Centre will supply and fit any kind of stove – they even sweep the chimneys. Central heating fuel can be supplied from the firm next door. Scottish Stone stocks all shapes, sizes and types of rock – a geologist's dream. The old Croftamie primary school is now a nursery, still starting children along the long road of education. Croftamie is a busy place.

National Cycle Route 7 passes through the village and the West Highland Way is on the doorstep, bringing extra hungry mouths to feed. The Wayfarers Restaurant is just the place. Mine host played a bit of football and is now a well known pundit. With Scotland ranked 88th in the world, perhaps he should still be playing!

D

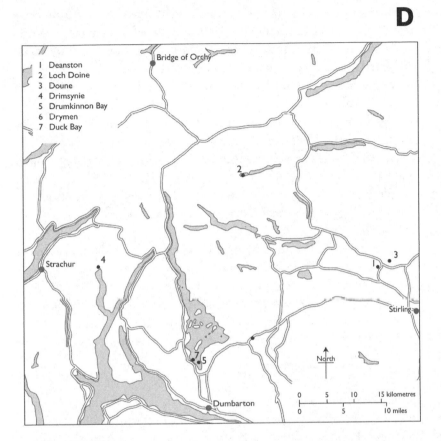

1 Deanston
2 Loch Doine
3 Doune
4 Drimsynie
5 Drumkinnon Bay
6 Drymen
7 Duck Bay

Deanston

Deanston can be said to be the Siamese twin of Doune, joined with it by the A84. It is the River Teith that separates them, allowing the development of quite different characters. Deanston is shy and retiring; hidden away behind the trees it really does have an identity of its own. Being so close to Doune, with its famous castle, tourists will mostly overlook Deanston, a place few people have heard of.

There are traces of settlement from the period 2500–700 BC,

the Bronze Age. The process of metalworking was probably controlled by a small number of people. By keeping control over the distribution of the metal, some families and groups became more influential, and a class structure became established. There was a move towards individual burial and the inclusion of valuable grave goods. A Bronze Age cairn lies close to the river bank.

Also bronze in colour, but quite different in nature, is the whisky produced at the Deanston distillery. The building was designed as a cotton mill by Richard Arkwright, pioneer of mechanical spinning, and dates from 1785. The mill closed in the early 1960s, becoming a distillery in 1965. Four floors had to be removed to accommodate the tall stills and the machinery. The unpeated single malt is available at 12 and 17 years old.

The River Teith, once used to power the old mills, is still being harnessed today. The same water that produces the whisky also drives two turbines, supplying all the electricity for the distillery. Surplus capacity is fed into the National Grid, and not a wind turbine in sight – yet. They recycle, too. Deanston whisky is left to mature in second hand bourbon and sherry casks.

Deer

Scotland is the last stronghold of Britain's largest wild animal – the red deer (*Cervus elaphus*). The Loch Lomond and Trossachs National Park is home to a large number of deer and recent high population counts have given cause for concern. Although nobody likes the thought of killing Bambi, there has to be an element of management and control. Culling of surplus stags and hinds provides an income and maintains a healthy stock.

Except at rutting in the autumn, stags live in small, bachelor herds. In the Highlands, large herds of hinds and young animals can be seen on the hillsides. In summer they usually keep to the higher ground, following the growth of new heather shoots and avoiding the attentions of biting flies. Cold summer nights and harsh winter weather bring the deer to lower ground and their true habitat – woodland.

High deer numbers cause problems for foresters, for farmers and for the deer themselves. In their search for food, hungry animals roam at large, damaging trees, crops and quite a few motorcars. The choice is simple, if unpleasant. Fence in the countryside or reduce the deer. With the new Countryside Access Act in place, fencing is not an option. The Forestry Commission, responsible for the Trossachs and Cowal Forest Districts, ensure that culling is carried out to the highest standards.

The National Park also has populations of sika, fallow and roe deer, with the odd sighting of muntjak. Sika are a real menace. Imported from Asia about 150 years ago, they freely cross with red deer, producing fertile hybrid offspring. Throughout this area there will be ample opportunity to see wild deer – stay quiet and keep your eyes open.

Loch Doine

Loch Doine is one of the jewels of the National Park. Its name means 'the Deep Loch' and it is squeezed between Meall Monachyle and Ceann na Baintighearna ('Her Ladyship's Head'). This 2,531 ft Corbett is home to eagles and to breathtaking scenery. For centuries this was the land of MacLaren, Ferguson, Stewart and MacGregor. It was here, at Monachyle Tuarach, that Rob Roy took his first farm, in 1692.

In the traditional manner, Rob would have begged his stock from his family and friends. Having established himself, the next year young Rob was able to marry his Mary, and set up home at Inversnaid. He left one of his men to run the farm at Loch Doine. The man was a MacDonald – a name that would come back and haunt him.

The first visit by Sir Walter Scott, as a Sheriff's Officer, almost ended in his death. However, Scott was so taken by this untamed country and its wild people that he returned time and again to collect material for his novels. One story used by Scott was about Donald MacLaren of Invernenty. En route to his execution at

Carlisle, MacLaren hurled himself from his mount into the Devil's Beef Tub, high above Moffat – and lived to tell the tale.

The six miles from Kingshouse to Loch Doine, under the Braes of Balquhidder, will seem much longer, but nowhere else will you find such beauty. At Monachyle Mhor there is food to match the scenery; an award-winning restaurant and working farm, it is in the hands of the second generation of the Lewis family. At breakfast the sun rises over one Ben Vorlich in the east, and at supper it sets behind another Ben Vorlich to the west. If there is heaven on earth, then this is it.

Doune

The Romans camped for a while at Doune, at the site of the present day primary school. This place name is simply from Gaelic *dun* – a fortress. A 6th century missionary called Doais settled here, giving his name to the area, Kilmadoc. Early Celtic fortification, at the confluence of the Teith and Ardoch waters, became a medieval castle, built for Robert, Duke of Albany. Many kings and queens have stayed within these walls.

The busy A84 from Stirling does not align well with the stone bridge at Doune. This was built at the behest of James Spittal, tailor to James IV. Spittal had been refused a crossing on the Teith ferry, and persuaded King James to fund a bridge. In no time at all, the poor ferryman was ruined – revenge indeed. Cyclists on National Route 76, Callander/Doune/Dunblane, have to run the gauntlet of traffic on this narrow, old bridge.

Doune became a centre for the shoeing of Highland cattle, passing through on their way to distant southern markets. At one time there were eight smithies at work in the town. In 1649, the discovery of how to turn worn-out shoe nails into blast-proof metal gave rise to a new industry – gun making. For the next 150 years, Doune pistols were acknowledged to be unmatched by any other.

Doune Castle was held for Bonnie Prince Charlie by the notorious wild MacGregors of Glengyle, but not so much as a hen went missing in the town during their stay. The castle has featured in many films and large numbers of Monty Python fans come in search of the Holy Grail. Other visitors scour Doune looking for antiques. There are pleasant trails in and around this hamlet, a monthly programme of guided walks and an annual walking festival.

Drimsynie

Drimsynie was a typical Argyllshire hill farm, running blackface sheep on the high ground and cattle on the lower slopes. Over the last 40 years, farmers have found their margins slashed and incomes drastically reduced. In 1960, 10 per cent of Scottish farmers were relying on ancillary business to survive, mainly providing accommodation. By the year 2000, that number had risen to a massive 90 per cent. It was a case of diversify or die.

At Drimsynie, originally rented from the Forestry Commission, they have developed an impressive tourist based industry. Agriculture is now integrated with a complex of hotels, chalets and caravans. A leisure centre has a swimming pool, steam and sauna rooms, as well as bowling and ice-skating – all in deepest Argyll. Outdoor enthusiasts can enjoy water activities, pony trekking, walks and climbs, and golf.

Drimsynie, also known as Campbell's Kingdom, sits at the head of Loch Goil. The Gaelic name may simply mean 'the Long Ridge' (*druim* – a ridge – and *sineidh* – stretching). However, if the second syllable is read as *sian*, that would mean 'a storm'. There certainly is a ridge running north from the sea, two miles long and 817 ft/249 m high. Looking down Loch Goil, there would certainly have been storms, too.

Apart from the sea, the only way in to Drimsynie is along six miles of single-track road. Surrounded by mountains, the natural isolation gives the area a certain attraction – especially for outlaws. It is claimed that Rob Roy hid in a cave at Drimsynie. In 10 years on the run, Rob had need to use all his secret caves and hiding places on a regular basis.

Drumkinnon Bay

Drumkinnon is at the southern tip of Loch Lomond, the third longest and third deepest loch in Scotland. Lomond, however, has the largest surface area of freshwater in Britain, over 27 square miles (70 sq km). At Drumkinnon, the waters rapidly funnel into the River Leven, the only outflow from the loch. From earliest times there has been settlement here; battles too. A Scots' incursion of 704 AD was beaten off with great slaughter.

Drumkinnon means 'the Ridge of the Rabbit'. Although wild rabbits were not recorded at Loch Lomond before 1825, rabbits would have been kept at Drumkinnon at an earlier date. Warrens and doocots would have soon been established by the incoming Anglo-Norman Earls of Lennox. These provided fresh rabbit and pigeon meat, even in the depths of winter, but only for the new aristocracy.

The moored *Maid of the Loch* is serving as a floating restaurant and conference centre while funding is put in place to finish her refit. Smaller vessels can be launched from the public slipway if they have registered with the Park Authority. Boats, canoes and bikes can be hired at Drumkinnon. Those preferring terra firma can simply enjoy the magnificent views, either from the shore or high up in the tower.

A modern interpretation of an ancient castle, Drumkinnon Tower is the centrepiece of the Loch Lomond Shores complex. The shops, restaurants and vast information centre cater for millions of visitors from all over the world. Young and old alike can learn about and appreciate the wonderful heritage of this loch – where the Highlands and Lowlands collide.

Drymen

Druim, with the diminutive ending *-in*, is Gaelic for 'ridge'. After the last Ice Age, 10,000 years ago, any dry land would have been at a premium. Early settlers here became known as the *Druimanach* – the

People of the Ridge. This ridge had the strategic advantage of over-looking the lowest fording point on the Endrick River. Situated close to two gateways into the Highlands, Drymen became one of the first tourist centres.

The Romans arrived in 84 AD, putting up a fort on the doorstep. The road builders were striking through to the west, skirting Loch Lomond, as part of the campaign of conquest. This excursion was short lived – the local Attacottii saw to that. Roman soldiers welcomed death in battle as the surest way to immortality and everlasting glory. However, they did not like the idea of being eaten for supper!

Margaret Atheling, granddaughter of the last Saxon king of England, came to Scotland to marry Malcolm III. The lands of Drymen were granted to one of her retainers, Maurice, a Hungarian nobleman. Maurice took the name of his new estate, becoming known as Drummond. Central administration and royal control was strengthened by a system of charters and grants of land. Feudal times had arrived.

Drymen developed as a livestock centre. A weekly Thursday market was set up by Act of Parliament in 1669. There were also two annual fairs, on 10 May and 15 October. At Drymen Show, at the end of May, there are echoes of those past times. In 1734, Rob Roy's sister took out a license for the Clachan Inn, one of seven hostelries in the village. There are still four today, including the Clachan. For those using the two golf courses nearby, there is no shortage of 19th holes. Dry men, never!

Duck Bay

Duck Bay is a small, sheltered bay, lying just north of Cameron Point, with anchorage available on both sides of the pier. These waters are the busiest on Loch Lomond, and the marina, hotel and restaurant provide every facility required by visitors and boating people. The frenetically busy A82 bypasses Duck Bay – access is via a short section of the old lochside road.

Duck Bay Marina had the reputation of being one of Scotland's top nightspots. At weekends loud music and dazzling lights would take over the nights. Today, everything is much more sedate – fine food and wine have become very much the order. The views from the restaurant are superb. Inside the dining room, another feature is well worth a close look. A map of Loch Lomond, wrought in metal, takes up the whole of one wall.

Duck Bay certainly has plenty of ducks, predominantly mallard, now quite recovered from the noisy intrusions of the past. The place name, however, has nothing to do with the local wildlife – it means 'Black Water'. *Dubh Uisge* has become contracted and rendered as 'Duck'. The burn flowing into the loch at Duck Bay carries water darkened with peat.

The panorama from Duck Bay is immense – north, up the loch, and deep into the Highlands. A line of wooded islands takes the eye a few points east, marking a great geological fault. This is the Highland Boundary. Directly east are the parklands of Balloch Castle. They are home to a large boulder, Pettie's Stone. This was the limit of the territory held by Paternius, a 5th century Pictish king. Perhaps he moored his birlin at Duck Bay!

E

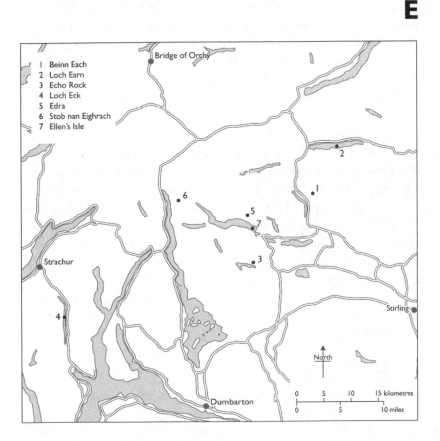

1 Beinn Each
2 Loch Earn
3 Echo Rock
4 Loch Eck
5 Edra
6 Stob nan Eighrach
7 Ellen's Isle

Bridge of Orchy

Strachur

Stirling

Dumbarton

North

0   5   10   15 kilometres
0   5   10 miles

Beinn Each

Beinn Each is a Corbett of 2,667 ft/813 m. Pronounced *Bin Yech*, the name translates into English as 'Horse Hill'. No ordinary horses these, but the greatly feared water spirits known as kelpies. The waters of the Highlands are believed to be inhabited by strange, mysterious and rather magical beasts. Most of these creatures are quite harmless and no threat to mankind. Kelpies, on the other hand, are said to be extremely dangerous.

The mountain stands over the 1,000 ft/300 m high pass between

Strathyre and Glen Ample. A steep track climbs from Ardchullarie Farm, through a forest, and into a narrow glen. After a mile or so, leave the path and make your own way up the south west slope to the summit. It is an incessant climb, all the way from Ardchullarie More, but the views from the top make it worthwhile.

Near here was the place known as the Shieling of the One Night. Many years ago, two young girls, one dark and one fair, both called Mairi, were to spend the night in a new-built bothy. Once the building had been completed, other young women would bring the children and livestock to the high summer pastures. This was the way of Highland life.

As the first light of morning began to filter through the unfinished thatch, the fair Mairi awoke to find the room full of horses. Her companion was lying half-eaten on the floor! When the poor girl was found, quite deranged by the horror, a herd of horses was seen disappearing into the dark waters of Lochan a Chroin.

It would seem that, when kelpies come out of the loch to feed, they look for just one thing – human flesh. Particularly young and female human flesh.

Loch Earn

Loch Earn is six miles from east to west and fifteen miles round by road. Home to various clubs and a water sports centre, the loch is one of the busiest stretches of water in Scotland. Wind surfers, water skiers and boats of all sorts make patterns across the surface, while fishermen line the wooded shores. *Earn* is believed to be a pre-Celtic name for a sacred water.

Where they saw water coming out of the ground, the earliest people thought they were looking at gods, coming up from the Underworld to bring life and sustenance. Water also gives protection. In troubled times past, women and children found refuge on the island retreats. Since 1957, these same waters have generated 78 million units of hydroelectricity every year. Loch Earn is certainly living up to its name.

On the south road there are two interesting stones. One marks the spot where the body of Stewart of Ardvorich was hidden from the wild MacGregors, bent on doing horrible things – even though he was already dead. The other stone indicates the final resting place of seven MacDonalds from Glencoe, who were killed raiding Ardvorlich cattle in 1620. The bodies had to be moved here during road widening – no rest for the wicked.

At the south west corner of the loch are the faint remains of St Blane's chapel and the imposing Edentaggart Castle. Shaggy Highland cattle graze the lochside fields. St Fillans, at the other end of Loch Earn, is picturesque and rather tranquil. After a hard day, this is just the place to relax, drink in hand, and watch the sun set behind the western hills.

Echo Rock

Three miles from Aberfoyle, along the wonderful B829, on the north side of Loch Ard, Echo Rock is well named. It was at this spot that Rob Roy MacGregor, being hotly pursued by Redcoats, opened his lungs and let out a mighty shout. After a few seconds, echoes came bouncing back from the encircling hills and the soldiers thought they had been led into an ambush and fled.

Here, too, worship was conducted in great secrecy at a time when it was deemed an act of treason to be a member of the Presbyterian Church. The congregation would gather in the lee of Echo Rock, while the minister preached from his pulpit stone on the other side of the water. A piper, stationed at the nearby Pass of Aberfoyle, would warn of approaching danger. At the sounding of the pipes, everyone would quickly disappear.

Beneath the pulpit is a small cave, one of many used by Rob Roy. Later it became the collecting point for the spirit distilled locally, which was poured into non-returnable French wine and brandy casks. This was just one of the benefits of the Auld Alliance! The raw spirit was brought to the cave in small flasks secreted in high-sided boots – hence, bootlegging. It would take some time to fill all the barrels, allowing the spirit to age and mature.

People still gather at the Echo Rock. It is a good place to launch kayaks and canoes, and to generally mess around in the water. Other people sit on the low stone wall and cast a fly on the loch, hoping for a fine brown trout. Still others simply admire the view. A few climbers face the challenge of the rock, seeming to defy the force of gravity. Now and again, someone will stop and shout and count the echoes.

Loch Eck

Loch Eck is 'the Loch of the Horse' – the mysterious *each uisge* or kelpie. It is also home to the elusive powan, sometimes referred to as a freshwater herring but actually one of the salmon family. Found in only a handful of British waters, the Loch Eck powan's nearest neighbours are in Loch Lomond. Powan are a reminder that these lochs were, long ago, open to the sea. Loch Eck is shallow, narrow and comparatively modest, but the setting is dramatic.

The six mile loch is tightly hemmed in by the surrounding mountains, which are often streaked with falling white water. The views constantly change with the moods of light and wind. A conspicuous outcrop of rock, on the north slope of Clach Bheinn, is seen locally as a praying monk. But the Gaels know it as *poit dubh* – the black pot or small still – as it resembles the distilling device, useful for producing a drop of special mountain dew.

One evening, as the mist began to gather, a crofter went away to his still. All the while he was looking out for one of his mares, which was newly foaled. Eventually he saw an animal in front of him that he took to be his mare. But as he approached, the creature suddenly reared up, now twice the size of a natural horse, and let out a fearful scream. The crofter took off for his life – and never stopped running until he was safely under his own roof. The waters of Loch Eck must be safer now; the loch is the main supply for Dunoon.

There are picnic sites dotted along the eastern shoreline, and many walks and cycle paths in the area. One of the finest walks follows the ancient drove road from the Whistlefield Inn, through the length of Glen Finart, to the sea at Loch Long. Over the years very little has changed.

Edra

Edra is an abbreviation of *Edraleachdach*, 'the Farm Between Two Stone-flagged Burns' – quite a mouthful in Gaelic or English. Edra is four miles from the Trossachs Pier, almost halfway along the north shore of Loch Katrine. No cars are allowed to use the Water Board road, but bicycles can be hired at the car park, or you can bring your own. The farm steading sits up on a ridge, a stone-flagged burn on either side.

Organically produced vegetables are being grown on the front fields. The native blackface sheep and suckler cows which so recently foraged here are gone. Nature is rapidly reclaiming her own. Red deer browse but make little impression, and wild flowers abound. Stroll along the loch shore, scramble up the burn sides or venture out the glen.

Edra is a bird watcher's paradise – everywhere you look there are birds to be seen, everything from the golden eagle, buzzard and hen harrier, right down to the tiny skylark and meadow pipit. In the summer months, golden plover cry plaintively on the high tops and coveys of grouse burst from underfoot. Amongst the trees, sparrowhawks pursue their quarry while the enormous capercailzie lies in wait. Anything entering his territory will be chased off, even man.

A mile or so out of the broad Edra glen, so wide that it is more of a strath, are the ruins of an old township. Each of these farming communities would have consisted of between three and twenty families, all living and working together – and, under the clan chief, fighting together. At the 1745 uprising, the Duke of Perth's standard-bearer came from Edra. The infamous Highland Clearances removed these people. Now a second Clearance has come to this glen.

Education

One of the four main aims of Scotland's first National Park is education. This is largely the responsibility of the Park Ranger Service, a full time dedicated team backed up by seasonal staff. To cover an area of 720 square miles, the Loch Lomond and Trossachs National Park has been divided into four sections: Argyll, Breadalbane, Loch Lomond and Trossachs, each with its own area office.

A wide-ranging syllabus has been developed to provide information and guidance to people living and working within the park boundaries. This also caters for the ever-growing number of visitors that the park attracts. In order to maintain a safe environment, the Ranger Service liaises with the three forces that each police part of the National Park.

Greater awareness is a priority. A comprehensive programme of almost 150 events has been designed to inform and entertain the public throughout the year. This message is taken further afield on the back of the Green Scene Road Show. Wildlife areas have been established under the long established Grounds For Learning scheme, implemented through schools. Pupils are able to study a wide range of topics and carry out a variety of projects. Youngsters are given further encouragement through the John Muir Awards. The tiny Trossachs primary school recently received the prestigious John Muir Discovery Award. Joining forces with the National Park Ranger Service, they developed a wildlife area within the school grounds.

The National Park Education Officer can be contacted on 01389 722000.

Stob nan Eighrach

Stacked amongst the high hills of the north east corner of Loch Lomond, Stob nan Eighrach may mean 'the Icy Peak' (from Gaelic *stob* – peak – and *eighreach* – icy). However, there are two other possibilities. If the name has been derived from *eagach* – jaggy – that would describe the peak nicely. But the local belief is that this is 'the Hill of Prayer', a reference to the nunnery once sited at the foot of the hill, and locals usually know best. The holy women must have delivered their prayers up in a loud voice – *eagheach* is the act of shouting.

This community of nuns was set up, in conjunction with the St Fillan priory, by Robert Bruce, after his victory at Bannockburn. These wise women were frequently consulted on secular as well as religious matters – and occasionally on judicial issues.

It was a rash legal judgement that brought about their demise. The case concerned a man accused of stealing his neighbour's new horse, a very serious offence. The alleged theft had taken place on the Sabbath, following a church service. After deliberation, the women came to the conclusion that the man had done nothing worse than sit up upon the horse, and ordered his release. The horse, however, was guilty of kidnapping the man on her back – and should be hanged forthwith!

If approaching Stob nan Eighrach from Glengyle, the remains of the Court House can be seen on the lower slope of Ben Ducteach. A climb of Stob nan Eighrach can also be made from the West Highland Way, three miles north from Inversnaid or three miles south from Inverarnan. The Ardlui ferry provides a shortcut, landing at the foot of the 2,011 ft/613 m mountain. This is definitely the steep side.

Ellen's Isle

Ellen's Isle is the largest island on Loch Katrine, lying about one mile from the Trossachs Pier. The only way to get ashore is to hire one of the small number of boats available during the fishing season. Originally known as *Eilean Morlach*, 'the Shaggy Isle', because the trees and shrubs grew unchecked by grazing animals, it was renamed after a local woman who defended her honour in the way of her lawless times.

During the war between Charles II and the forces of the English

Parliament, a detachment of Roundheads was making its way along the north shore of the loch, burning and pillaging as it went. After darkness fell, one of the soldiers decided to swim out to the island, refuge of the women and children, full of evil intent. He came in quietly between a couple of boats, moored half in and half out of the water. As he poked his head up to have a look around, Ellen Stewart cut it off with one blow of a claymore!

The decapitated body was recovered by his comrades and lies buried in a little defile, still referred to as the Pass of the Stranger. Forgotten he may be, but he is never alone. Every day people stroll out from the car park at the Trossachs Pier, an easy walk with glorious views. In the dead of night, the animals of the forest walk over his grave.

Ellen's Isle is a haven for wildlife, mostly left quite undisturbed. In early springtime, the common gull returns to breed. In spite of its name it is not a common gull at all. Otters occasionally visit the island and ospreys fish in the water. How moles managed to get to Ellen's Isle is a mystery, but they are certainly in residence. Another creature said to put in an appearance is the Tarbh – the water bull from the depths of the loch.

F

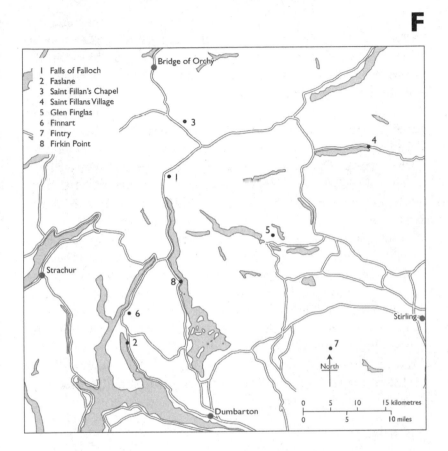

1 Falls of Falloch
2 Faslane
3 Saint Fillan's Chapel
4 Saint Fillans Village
5 Glen Finglas
6 Finnart
7 Fintry
8 Firkin Point

Faeries

The whole of Scotland, but especially the Highlands, is rich in folklore, legends and place names associated with the Little People. Faeries come in many guises and are usually kind in nature, although some are definitely not. Through their supernatural powers, faeries can become invisible at will. When seen, Highland faeries are fair, while those of the Lowlands are dark in complexion.

In the olden days, every family was assisted in its daily chores by little helpers, known as brownies. But you can have too much of a good thing. Trying to control the energy of these indefatigable beings became ever more difficult. In the Trossachs, the problem was solved when, in 1298, the abbot of Inchmahome banished the faeries from Menteith, leaving the area between Stirling and Aberfoyle a faerie-free zone.

The Little People had to pack up all their goods and chattels, and leave the area. Some crossed over to the west of the River Forth. Others went to the north, to live in the solitude of Balquhidder and Lochearnhead. The rest moved into the upper reaches of Strathard, which is why there are more faeries living at Loch Chon than any-where else in the world. You may find one or two employed in the local hotels.

Faerie stories span the centuries; certainly not all are locked in the distant past. One night, less than 90 years ago, a shepherd at Loch Katrine came upon a faerie ceilidh. After many hours of music and dancing, completely enchanted, he accepted an invitation to the Faerie Realm. But he found his entry to the other world barred by his possession of a single horseshoe nail made of iron. When he grasped hold of the nail to remove it from his person, a great force threw him to the ground. Recovering his breath, he found all was silent and the faeries were gone. The scar of that nail, seared into the palm of his hand, was carried to his grave.

Falls of Falloch

Falaichte means 'Hidden', from Gaelic *falaich* – to hide – and the Falls of Falloch are certainly hidden from view. From a small car park, on the east side of the road through Glen Falloch, a short walk will take you to the largest falls on this river. With an annual rainfall of 120 inches/3 m, you will hear the water of the Falloch cascading 30 ft into Rob Roy's Bath Tub long before the falls comes into sight.

This is a densely wooded glen that links the north end of Loch Lomond with the high country of Breadalbane, an ancient Celtic earldom. Through this narrow pass have come countless cattle droves, red-coated soldiers, shepherds and hillwalkers. Today there is the constant roar of traffic. Still visible are some sections of the old military road, built by James Wolfe of Quebec fame, running parallel with the busy A82.

Wolfe and his 4th Regiment of Foot had been posted to the Inversnaid Garrison with a double remit – build roads and quell MacGregors. At building roads Wolfe and his men excelled – some of their bridges here are still in heavy daily use. But when it came to dealing with Clan Gregor, Wolfe was an abject failure. And what do the English do with their great failures? They promote them – and the rest, as they say, is history.

On the open hillside, a stone's throw from the falls, stands Clach nam Breatann, a large boulder which marked the northern limit of British Strathclyde. The Scots, coming from the west, soon took this land for themselves. To the east, the Picts held on until 843 AD, when Kenneth MacAlpin finally united both kingdoms. It probably rained as much in those days as it does today, sending water plunging over the Falls of Falloch.

Faslane

Faslane lies in the waters of the Gare Loch, sheltered from the Atlantic swell by a pair of terminal moraines. This is the rubble left by a decaying glacier, 10,000 years ago. The gap between these moraines, through which the tides ebb and flow, has been widened to allow better access to the naval base. Faslane is a place where cattle droves were rested. Its name derives from Gaelic *fas* – a stance – and *lainne* – a field. Today it is a busy port.

Faslane has a long naval tradition. In 1764, there were 27 men of the parish serving in the Senior Service. During World War II, Faslane provided almost two and a half miles of deep-water quay and a marshalling yard with 22 miles of railway track. Now the trains skirt the modern submarine base which, together with Coulport, cost £1.7bn and took eight years to complete.

The base commands an annual budget of £267m and employs a workforce of around 6,250, divided equally between civilian and navy personnel. At any one time, 2,000 crewmembers will be ashore, many from the nuclear submarine fleet. Meanwhile, across the road, the colourful Peace Camp has been protesting against all weapons of mass destruction since 1982. One of their psychedelic caravans is in a Glasgow museum.

Not much remains of the original Faslane. The fine castle of the Earls of Lennox, frequented by Wallace and Bruce, is no more than an obscure mound. The ruins of St Michael's Church, built on a faerie hill, stand in the secluded burial ground. Here, the future Lord Darnley, father of James VI, was baptised. Here, too, lie the 30 men who lost their lives when submarine K13 sank, undergoing sea trials, in January 1917.

Saint Fillan's Chapel

Strathfillan was formed by a massive glacier which ploughed over the landscape between Ben Lui and Loch Tay. From time immemorial, this trough has been recognised as one of the main east-west links across the Highlands. In the heart of Strathfillan is the monastic site at Kirkton Farm, a mile south of Tyndrum. Walkers on the West Highland Way pass through the ruins of this ancient settlement, known as Saint Fillan's.

Faolan, an Irish proper name, meaning 'Little Wolf', was the name of 16 saints. This St Fillan came from Ireland with his mother, St Kentigerna, in the eighth century. After many years of wandering, Fillan eventually settled here, at a small monastery. He spent his last years writing out the Scriptures in the local dialect. To enable Fillan to illuminate his manuscripts, in more ways than one, his left arm miraculously glowed!

On the run and desperate for shelter, Robert Bruce found sanctuary with this group of monks in 1306. The newly crowned king of Scots was so taken with the mummified but still fluorescent forearm that he had it transferred to the cathedral at Dunblane. On the eve of Bannockburn, this same sacred relic mysteriously appeared in Bruce's tent. This gave the Scots heart, to take on and defeat the largest English army ever to come north.

There are many walks to enjoy around Saint Fillan's; along the banks of the nascent water of the Tay, here called the Fillan, or taking in some of the long-distance footpath. The walled burial ground has several old graves of interest. Nearby, a second graveyard has two fine yew trees and the healing waters of the Priest's Well. The adventurous can tackle Beinn Challum's 3,363 ft/1,025 m. This is Breadalbane – the High Country of Scotland.

St Fillans Village

St Fillans is regarded as one of Scotland's well kept secrets. The neat village is set in the magnificent scenery of Loch Earn and was originally known as Port of Lochearn. The old clachan was made up of just a few cottages and a limekiln, but managed to support both a brewery and a distillery. Today the village is a little longer, with several fine hotels and a hydroelectric power station.

To the south, on the craggy summit of Dundurn, St Fillan established his eighth century stronghold. Those early days of Christianity were dangerous times, indeed. Evidence of this occupation still survives and the water from the well is said to cure infertility. Below Dundurn, also called Dunfillan ('Fillan's Fort'), lies a superb nine hole golf course and the final resting place of the Stewarts of Ardvorlich.

The history is steeped in clan blood. Stewarts, MacGregors, MacDonalds, Drummonds and MacLarens were all involved, but the greatest protagonists of all were the Neishes and MacNabs. In 1532 a bitter clash between these two clans saw the last Neish fall at the Rude Stone. The stone, in Glen Baltican, is still stained with the victim's blood, and is now called the Red Stone.

The Neishes recovered, and by the early 17th century were living by plunder alone. On the last night of 1612, the MacNabs managed to surprise their great foes in their island retreat. The severed head of the Neish chief became incorporated into the clan crest of the MacNabs. A goose, which failed to give any warning of the attack, is commemorated by an oak tree growing in front of the Drummond Arms. That goose was so pampered, it lived until 1818!

Glen Finglas

Glen Finglas, the Glen of White Water, was a long-time hunting estate of Stewart kings and queens. In 1955, these white waters were gathered behind a new dam to augment Glasgow's water supply, becoming a feeder for Loch Katrine. A hydroelectric generating station was built into the system – a quiet, efficient and environmentally friendly way to produce power. And not a wind turbine to spoil the skyline.

The Woodland Trust acquired Glen Finglas in 1996 and removed the blackface sheep from the hills. This 10,200 acre (4,000 hectare) demesne is the largest and most ambitious project of the Trust. In the fullness of time, they hope to link the existing fragments of the ancient hunting forest and form one of the largest native woodlands in Scotland. This will eventually cover over half of Glen Finglas.

The Woodland Trust definitely has a visitor friendly policy. Many footpaths have been laid in, and new car parks are under construction. Parking is also available at the Brig o' Turk; refreshments too. From the licensed tearoom, the entire circuit of Glen Finglas is 14.5 miles (23 km), with a total elevation of 1,650 ft/500 m.

On the west side of the reservoir is a low mound with a few trees, sometimes seen as an island. This is the site of an old hunting lodge. Nearby, a long time ago, two hunters were settling down for the night in a humble bothy. They were paid a visit by two very beautiful women who, after some supper, suggested a walk under the stars. Only one of the men went out of that hut – never to be seen again.

Sir Walter Scott refers to the 'Green Women of Glen Finglas' who lure men to their demise, so be very careful who you stop to speak to!

Finnart

Finnart is Gaelic for 'the White Point or Promontory', on account of the white quartz exposed on the shoreline. Throughout history people have maintained a toehold beneath the towering hills. It is recorded that on his marriage to a Stewart of Lennox, Sir John Colquhoun received all the lands from Rahane to Finnart. Three hundred years later, in the 1830s, two fine mansions were built close to Loch Long. This was just the start.

The next big change to hit Finnart was getting underway in Glasgow. James Young was beginning to refine mineral oil from coal, patenting his discovery in 1850. When it was shown that this system could also refine crude oil from the ground, the oil hunt was on. Nine years later, the first significant oil strike was made, in Pennsylvania. In 1861, the oil rolled ashore in England, coming by the barrel. Soon oil was pouring in from many other countries around the world.

In May 1950, Finnart became part of the oil boom – a deep-water tanker terminal was under construction, and a steel pipeline was to run from Finnart to Grangemouth, 57 miles, right across the country. Two pumping stations were required, one at the terminal, the other at Balfron. Huge tankers began to slip into Loch Long, discharging 2.2 million tons of crude oil every year; by 1959, a new jetty and extra holding tanks had increased the annual capacity to 3.25 million tons. And the ships were about to get even bigger.

Nowadays the super tankers still have plenty of room to manoeuvre and more than enough water under the keel. Elaborate precautions have been taken to prevent any oil seepage; the environment is well protected. Most of the complex has been landscaped and is well hidden by trees. The little that can be seen is a small price to pay for all the benefits received by modern society.

Fintry

Fintry is a picturesque village in the heart of the old earldom of Lennox. Every summer Fintry is festooned with flowers, and it has many Britain in Bloom awards to its credit. The village is snuggled into a hollow on the banks of the Endrick Water, sheltered from the north by the Fintry Hills and from the south by the Campsie Fells. These ancient volcanic hills hold a few surprises – even seams of coal.

The name Fintry comes from two roots: Scots Gaelic *fionn* – white – and Brythonic *tref* – a homestead. This latter word, *tref*, would still be recognised by a Welsh speaker today. There has been settlement here for a very long time. Culcreuch Castle, once home to the Galbraiths, who had close connections to the Earls of Lennox, is now a popular hotel. Their clan tartan is worn by the United States Air Force pipe band.

Over the centuries the Endrick Water has supplied people and their livestock with drinking and cleaning water, powered mills, and provided a haven for wildlife. The river supports a varied population of birds, animals, plants and fish. This is an important spawning area for salmon, sea trout, brown trout and the strange, parasitic lamprey. Uniquely, Endrick lampreys never return to the sea, going no further than Loch Lomond, where they seek out the powan.

Fintry is renowned for two aspects of community life – the quality of its amateur dramatic productions, and its sport. Of all the many activities in the village, rugby has the highest profile. Irrespective of the vicissitudes of league campaigns, a recent appearance in the semi-final of the Scottish Cup has earned the Fintry Rugby Club a place in history. The hospitality in the Fintry Sports Club is pretty good, too.

Firkin Point

Halfway along the west shore of Loch Lomond, just off the busy road, is a surprisingly peaceful picnic area. Firkin is a small delta, a promontory built up by centuries of sediment laid down by a burn. All this soil was washed off the slopes of Beinn Bhreac. Long ago, this oasis of lush pasture was a magnet to the local deer, giving it the name *Feidh Ceann* – 'Deer Point'.

At the moment this site has one major drawback – its gates. These have been locked relatively early on summer evenings, and not opened at all during the winter, stopping people from getting in. (I am sure the deer had no such access problems.) Buses are totally excluded. Those fortunate enough to get off the road and down into Firkin picnic zone will find good toilets and plenty of information. A long stretch of old tarmac makes for easy walking and allows the pushing of buggies.

The narrowing loch, hemmed in by the Highlands, has had its depth measured at 650 ft – this was not quite at its deepest point, but was quite close to the bottom. Opposite the loch, the oak woodlands of Craig Royston cover the lower flanks of Ben Lomond – headless at this point. Walk south towards Rubha Mor and the 3,195 ft/974 m summit soon appears. Several small bays provide pleasant anchorage. Northwards, the fjord is dominated by Ben Vorlich.

From Firkin Point it is a short climb to an enchanted spot, a legendary faerie loch. At Lochan Uaine the Little People would dye the cloth of the local weavers. All was well until someone asked for some black cloth to be changed to white. Failing in this task, the faeries departed. Also at Firkin is an ancient yew, on the west side of the A82, under which Robert Bruce once slept.

Forestry

Forestry Commission Scotland is responsible for an enormous area of land, both within and around the National Park. The outline of the combined Argyll and Queen Elizabeth Forest Parks is remarkably similar to that of the Loch Lomond and Trossachs National Park. Together with a number of private woodland schemes, forestry is one of the largest rural employers.

Since the first plantings of 1929, much of the forest has reached harvesting age. Around 200,000 tonnes are removed each year and the process has become highly mechanised. One machine, costing a cool £275,000, is capable of felling, trimming and cutting a tree into required lengths, in well under a minute. The timber is mainly pulped for paper and chipboard or made into pallets, though some is used in construction.

Greater efforts are now being made to properly landscape the forest, breaking up the straight lines and monotonous cover of earlier plantations. Replanting takes into account underlying landforms, as well as colour, texture and scale. Some areas will be left open or only planted with native broadleaf trees. In future the forest will develop better habitats for wildlife and an ever-widening range of recreational activities.

The Forestry Commission has opened up its forests, permitting public access wherever possible. Many of the footpaths have been waymarked and, in some places, trees have been removed to clear the views. Forest drives have been established and a few off-road events introduced. Camping and caravanning are encouraged, and you can stay in a log cabin. Mountain bikes, quad bikes, horses and huskies all find facilities in the forest. In the words of the Commission's Active Woods scheme: get out, get the benefit.

G

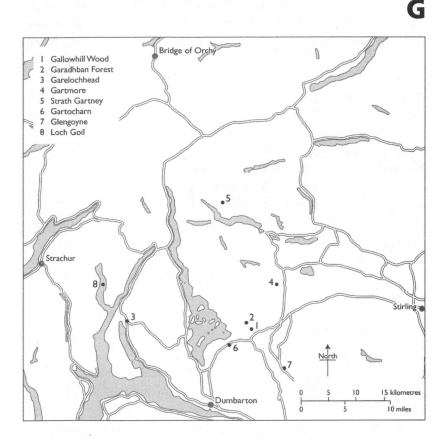

1 Gallowhill Wood
2 Garadhban Forest
3 Garelochhead
4 Gartmore
5 Strath Gartney
6 Gartocharn
7 Glengoyne
8 Loch Goil

Bridge of Orchy

Strachur

Stirling

North

Dumbarton

0   5   10   15 kilometres
0   5   10 miles

Gallowhill Wood

On the northern outskirts of Drymen, just off the road to Gartmore, stands Gallowhill Wood. The ancient trees are largely broadleaf, with a few tall Scots pines growing in one corner, and are under the care of Stirling Council. A gallows did indeed stand here in olden days – the ghost of one of its victims is said to wander the woods at night, rope burns clearly visible around her neck.

A network of well-made and relatively level paths makes Gallowhill Wood ideal for prams, pushchairs and wheelchair users.

Children cycle the paths in complete safety, well away from traffic, and build dens in the dark undergrowth. The amenity value of this remnant of 17th century coppiced woodland is supported by active management.

Gallowhill Wood nestles in a small triangle between Drymen primary school, some of the houses of the village and a farm. Over these fields, in the summer months, red shorthorn cattle graze – one of our rare native breeds. A traditional drystone dyke separates the wood from the farmland, and has a little ecosystem all of its own. Not much has changed here for a very long time.

The wood attracts many visitors. The local school children conduct environmental studies and have been known to win awards for their efforts. Bird and bat boxes have been put up by the pupils, as part of a long term project with the Countryside Rangers. Whether carpeted with spring flowers or glowing in autumnal colours, Gallowhill Wood is a haven for wildlife and a place of peace and tranquillity.

Garadhban Forest

Garadhban means 'the Hideout of the Women', from Gaelic *garadh* – a den, shelter or lair – and *ban*, genitive plural of *bean* – of the women. A mile north of Drymen, well out of the village, this could have been a refuge in times of trouble – or a secret place to practice black arts. Who knows what went on on this blasted heath, long before the first trees were planted?

This forest of alien spruces and larch was planted during the 1970s and truly envelops four miles of the West Highland Way. The excellent Forestry Commission road makes for pleasant walking and the handy car park attracts a number of horse riders and cyclists. Now and then the tall trees give way to tantalising views of distant hills and the island-speckled waters of Loch Lomond.

Over the coming years, as mature trees are harvested, native species such as oak, birch, rowan and Scots pine will be encouraged to grow. This will produce a natural forest, with a richer mix of ground-covering plants and more varied wildlife. Found throughout Europe, the Scots pine, *Pinus sylvestris*, is our only native conifer – the yew and juniper both produce flowers and berries, not cones.

When walking in the Garadhban Forest, some of nature's closest secrets may be revealed. The rare sika deer, introduced from eastern Asia, can occasionally be seen. Stags mark out their territories by thrashing bushes and fraying trees with their antlers. The autumnal rutting call is a distant whistle, repeated several times. Sika stags also blow rude raspberries!

Garelochhead

Garelochhead is Gaelic for 'the Head of the Short (*gearr*) Loch', an arm of the Clyde estuary. The sheltered water, protected by a terminal moraine between Rhu and Rosneath, provide safe anchorage and good sailing conditions. Large military vessels and stealthy nuclear submarines tie up at the Faslane Naval Base. Garelochhead surveys it all.

The beautiful prospects down to the Clyde are enhanced by a stunning backdrop of Highland mountains. To the west, beyond Loch Long, the high ridge is known as Argyll's Bowling Green, a rough English rendition of *Buaile-an Grian*, meaning 'Sunny Cattle Fold'. Perhaps by coincidence, it is said that the bloodthirsty Earls of Argyll would invite their adversaries to discuss any differences over a gentle game of bowls at this very place. The *bools* would, of course, have been the heads of their guests.

The hills rising to the east are also steeped in blood and gruesome deeds. In 1603, Colquhoun of Luss gathered a large force, including government troops, and set out to attack the MacGregors. Colquhoun came face to face with the wild Highlanders sooner than he expected, in Glen Fruin – the Glen of Weeping. More than 300 men of Luss perished, for the loss of only two MacGregors. But Clan Gregor was about to be outlawed for the next 171 years.

There is still a strong military presence in the area, with miles of barbed wire and high, forbidding fences. Even with these severe restrictions, there are many fine walks to enjoy around here. Train and bus services link with Garelochhead and refreshments can be found in a couple of pubs and an extremely good tearoom.

Gartmore

Gartmore was a 17th century township or fermtoun, which served the needs of the drovers bringing their cattle out of the Highlands. The main route down Strathard and through Aberfoyle would soon arrive at Gartmore. The name of the village simply means 'the Big Field or Enclosure' in which the cattle would be rested. It is known that Rob Roy MacGregor frequently bought cattle at Gartmore Fairs.

The present village was laid out in the 18th century and is one of the best examples of estate planning. The first tenant was a brewer. He was soon followed by a shoemaker, a cartwright, a tailor, a surgeon, several merchants and a minister. The Black Bull, still famous for fine food, dates from 1700. The school was built in 1719 and the church in 1790. The priorities of the laird are quite evident.

Gartmore House, designed by William Adam, was built for the Cunninghame Graham family and set in 75 acres of unspoiled countryside. The last, and one of the greatest in his line, was the colourful R.B. Cunninghame Graham – Don Roberto. He was in turn, a Liberal MP – first president of the Scottish Labour Party – and founder of the National Party for Scotland. The monument to this writer, politician and Argentinean gaucho stands at the football field. His body rests in the ruins of Inchmahome Priory.

For several years the village shop has been owned and success-fully run by the community. As both the National Cycle Route 7 and the long-distance Rob Roy Way pass through Gartmore, there are plenty of extra customers. There are good walks in and around the village, some linking up to the Queen Elizabeth Forest Park.

Strath Gartney

'Strath' is a term used for a wide, flat river valley, though here it is more akin to the Irish sense of a lochside meadow. Both these descriptions perfectly fit Strath Gartney, but I prefer a more local explanation – a personal name. Gartnait was an 8th century Pictish chief who held out against the Scots invaders as they expanded their new kingdom of Dalriada ever eastward.

Strath Gartney sweeps from the fastness of the Highlands and runs the full length of Loch Katrine, Scotland's twelfth largest loch and Glasgow's main reservoir. It was to the safety of this strath that the fugitive Clan Gregor came in 1533. Harried from pillar to post by more powerful clans, particularly the mighty Campbells, Strath Gartney became their refuge. The most famous son of that clan, Rob Roy MacGregor, was born in the strath, at Glengyle, in 1660.

Tourism descended upon Strath Gartney in 1810, following the publication of Sir Walter Scott's epic poem, 'The Lady of the Lake'. His story unfolded a world of fantasy, myth and legend – and people flocked to the Trossachs. The seal of royal approval was appended in October 1859, when Queen Victoria opened the sluices to send pure Highland water to the city of Glasgow.

The best way to see Strath Gartney is from the deck of ss *Sir Walter Scott*, sailing during the summer season from the Trossachs Pier. The south side mountains tumble steeply into the loch. The high ground to the north, however, gives way to half a dozen small farms, strung along the strath like beads. The stonewalled fields lie empty and the surrounding hills remain ungrazed. In July 2002, Scottish Water abandoned farming and cleared the high ground and the glens.

Gartocharn

Gartocharn is 'the Place of the Humped Hill', from *garradh* – place or enclosure – and *chairn* – a humped hill – a corrupted form of *cairn*. The humped hill is a well known landmark – Duncryne – usually referred to as 'the Dumpling'. At only 465 ft/142 m, Duncryne is the most prominent feature along the south shore of Loch Lomond. The views from the top, into the heart of the Highlands, are quite amazing.

The earliest imprint of man in Scotland, a hearth site, was found at Gartocharn. At that time Loch Lomond was open to the sea. During the hard winter months, the nomadic tribes would settle at the seaside and eke out a living from the unfrozen waters. The Lang Cairn is a burial mound dating from the Stone Age. Some of the gods were thought to dwell amongst the sacred aspen trees, at the top of Duncryne. That was a long time ago.

The centre of the village is around the church, the new Millennium Hall and France Farm – originally laid out as an exact map of our partner in the Auld Alliance. Prime beef cattle from France Farm have taken fatstock prizes up and down the land. On two occasions they brought home the prestigious Smithfield Championship from London. Fresh produce is sold at the farm every Friday, alongside the crafts available in the hall.

The old Gartocharn Inn was built about the middle of the nineteenth century, to slake the thirst of the quarrymen hewing out the red sandstone. Once the social hub of the community, it is now the Hungry Monk, serving good food but somewhat pricey. It is the small village shop, catering for local needs and passing trade, that has become the social and information centre of Gartocharn.

Glengoyne

Glengoyne is 'the Valley of the Geese', tucked into the foot of the Campsie Fells, eight miles north of Milngavie. The tiny hamlet of Drumgoyne, with a handful of houses, a post office, an inn and a distillery, is usually the first resting place on the long walk to Fort William, the West Highland Way. A little excursion to the top of the Earl's Seat, 1,876 ft/578 m, is well worth the effort.

It was here that Rob Roy was almost captured by the Redcoats, once again slipping through their grasp. Rob had spent the day dealing in cattle and wrestling in the tournaments at the Milngavie Fair. He was quite an adversary, even without his sword. With the troopers right on his heels, the fugitive slipped inside an old, hollow ash tree and could not be found.

Glengoyne is one of the most picturesque distilleries. The neat, whitewashed buildings and the classical pagoda roof on the kiln belie the fact that this is an industrial unit. At Glengoyne, unpeated malt, from Golden Promise barley, is conjured into used Palo Cortado sherry casks and matured for many years. Because the all-important water emanates from the distant mountains, these single malts are all classified as 'Highland'.

At one time, long ago, when this whisky was known as Glen Guin, much of it was taken secretly to Glasgow. There it was stored and blended in the basement of the Free Church, at the Broomielaw. One thing is for certain – the minister must have been a man of taste and discernment.

Loch Goil

The translation of Loch Goil is usually given as 'the Loch of the Stranger', from the Gaelic *gall*. Early Irish uses the same word to mean foreigner. An alternative suggestion is that the name comes from one of the sons of Fergus Mor MacErc – Congall. Fergus Mor, son of Erc, led a group of settlers from Antrim, just across the sea, at the end of the 5th century. These people were known as *Scotti*, or Scots.

The well-sheltered waters of Loch Goil are excellent for sailing – many yachts and small boats take full advantage of the six mile stretch, surrounded by magnificent mountain scenery. On the north side of the Firth of Clyde, the hidden entrance to Loch Goil is clearly marked by the flashing light of Carraig nan Ron, a tiny island on the west side of Loch Long.

The water of Loch Goil is usually calm and tranquil, but not always. At one time the nearest lifeboat was stationed at far away Campbeltown. Today, the rescue services, coordinated from Fort

Matilda, near Greenock, are much closer at hand. Modern technology and a Coastguard communication network will ensure a rapid response to any incident, no matter how small.

There is no pier at Lochgoilhead, but once ashore, supplies, refreshments and, if required, medical attention can be found. Once the sun is over the yardarm, a welcoming drink can be enjoyed at Carrick Castle. This is a replacement – the original castle was destroyed by fire in 1685. This is one of the quietest corners of the National Park, long favoured by wealthy Glaswegians, who built the later mansions that line the shores of Loch Goil.

H

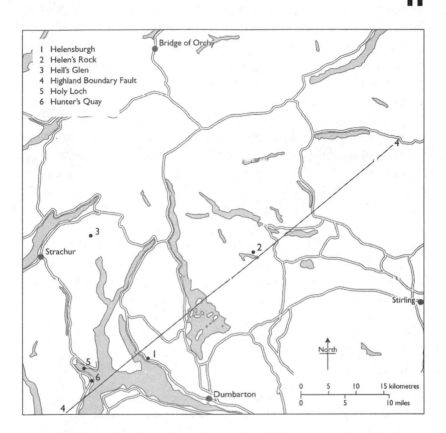

1 Helensburgh
2 Helen's Rock
3 Hell's Glen
4 Highland Boundary Fault
5 Holy Loch
6 Hunter's Quay

Bridge of Orchy

Strachur

Stirling

Dumbarton

North

0   5   10   15 kilometres
0   5   10 miles

Helensburgh

Helensburgh was founded on 11 January 1776, when Sir James Colquhoun of Luss announced a New Town, in the *Glasgow Journal*, for bonnet makers, stocking knitters and weavers of wool and linen. A quarry was available to provide stone for building, and adequate grazing for milk cows would be provided. It was originally called Muleig (Malig or Milrigs), then New Town and, finally, Helensburgh – after the wife of Sir James.

The most spectacular approach is from Loch Lomond, along the B832, looking down into the Firth of Clyde. Flanked by the wooded peninsulas of Rosneath and Ardmore, with the mountains of Arran on the southern skyline, the wide estuary is always busy. Constantly criss-crossing the water are squadrons of sailing boats, naval vessels making their way to or from the Gare Loch, cargo carriers bound for Glasgow, luxury liners to Greenock, and myriad ferries.

Helensburgh has a wide variety of hotels, restaurants, pubs, cafés and coffee shops. There is a continental touch in the main square – outside tables. For the actively inclined, there are excellent facilities at the town swimming pool and fitness centre. Helensburgh has golf, rugby, bowling, cricket, football and, of course, sailing. Everywhere people seem to be out jogging, morning, noon and night. Did I mention the chiropractor?

Walks include the gentle paths of Duchess Wood and the harder Upland Way – which passes the famous Hill House, designed in every detail by Charles Rennie Mackintosh. The seafront promenade has memorials to John Logie Baird, inventor of television, and Henry Bell, who built the first sea-going steamboat, the *Comet*. Bell's obelisk is the tallest single piece of Peterhead granite.

Helen's Rock

Helen's Rock is a precipitous drop into Loch Ard, off the south side of Dun Dubh. This guards the approach to the Pass of Aberfoyle, one of only four entries into the Scottish Highlands. It was here, in 83 AD, that the Romans built a small fort – a natural block to protect the main camp, four miles to the south. Helen's Rock is supposed to be named after the wife of Rob Roy MacGregor, although she was really called Mary.

The mistake was that of Sir Walter Scott, who confused this story with the one told about Ellen's Isle, and simply mixed up the two MacGregor women. It was Mary who called out the clan from Glengyle, after her husband had been lifted by Redcoats. Near Loch Ard, they encountered another army patrol and, after a short skirmish, captured a young officer. In order to extract information, the unfortunate soldier was dangled over a drop, and Mary threatened to cut the rope. Rob was soon reunited with his wife and his loyal clansmen, and the Hanoverian officer was sent on his way – quite unharmed.

With the publication in 1817 of Scott's *Rob Roy*, in which he misnames the wife of our hero, many now believe her to be Helen, Helen-Mary or Mary-Helen. All quite wrong – she was only ever Mairi.

Hell's Glen

This used to be the main route from Invereray, and the heartlands of deepest Argyll, to Glasgow. The greater part of such journeys would have been over water. When you see some of the rugged land that people had to traverse, it is clear why water was the preferred option. Sweeping chicanes and alpine bends lift both ends of the B839, as it fights its way through Gleann Beag ('Small Glen') – otherwise known as Hell's Glen.

The name was well chosen by the 18th century road builders. It is just three miles as the crow flies, but appreciably longer on the ground. Those men must have thought that they were labouring at the very gates of Hades! All around about them, charcoal burners filled the air with acrid smoke and, at night, eerie fires illuminated the forest.

But charcoal was important stuff. In the 18th century it was used for many purposes, primarily the smelting of iron. Early smelting was carried out at small sites, known as Bloomeries, scattered through the glens, where the ore and wood were both at hand. Later, smelting became more concentrated. The nearest centre was at Furnace, on Loch Fyne. Charcoal was also used to make gunpowder, to create big bangs – and to test the proof of whisky.

Hell's Glen is hemmed in by Cruach nam Mult (1,981 ft/610 m) to the south and Stob an Eas (2,376 ft/731 m) on the north side. Even the trees seem to be crowding onto the road. The way forward is blocked by the Brown Hill, Ben Donich, a massive 2,771 ft/845 m. Here the road turns south, joins the B828 as it comes out of neighbouring Gleann Mor (Big Glen), and follows the River Goil to the sea at Lochgoilhead.

Highland Boundary Fault

The geology of Scotland is anything but simple and can be traced back over 600 million years. The natural processes that have shaped the landscape still continue, almost imperceptibly, to reshape our world – wind, rain, frost, river erosion and occasional small earthquakes. The impact of these forces depends largely on the characteristics of the rocks being affected.

The major geological feature in this part of Scotland is the Highland Boundary Fault, which came into being some 450 million years ago. At that time two landmasses collided, bulldozing between them a layer of marine mud full of well-rounded stones and boulders. This is known as pudding stone, for quite obvious reason, and can be seen running in a straight line from Helensburgh to Stonehaven.

North of the fault line are the hard ancient rocks, laid down as ocean sediment 600 million years ago, at the very beginning of our story. Extreme heat and enormous pressure reformed the rock, and geological movement forced the whole lot up into a new range of mountains as high as Everest is today. But even these hard, metamorphic rocks are subject to the forces of nature, and are now weathered down to mere rumps of their former glory.

Soft sedimentary rocks are confined to the south of the Highland Boundary Fault. These mainly comprise a thick layer of old red sandstone, deposited about 380 million years ago. At the same time there was a period of great volcanic activity, just to enliven the picture. The precision of the fault line can be seen in the perfect alignment of the islands across Loch Lomond. The best place to explore the fault is at the David Marshall Lodge, Aberfoyle. A waymarked route has been created, with storyboards to explain the geological feature.

Holy Loch

Three Highland glens emerge into Strath Eachaig: Eck, Massan and Lean fuse together before dipping into the Holy Loch. In Gaelic this is *Loch Seanta*, the 'Enchanted or Magical Water', and this area is certainly one of early religious significance. St Fintan, of Teach in Ireland, founded a church at Kilmun, on the north side of the loch, in the 7th century. But when a vessel laden with sand from the Holy Land, for the building of Glasgow Cathedral, became stranded upon these shores, the loch's reputation was made.

A later church, built by the Campbells of Lochaw in 1442, became the final resting place of their clan chiefs. The rent due was a yearly payment of a pair of Parisian gloves, if asked for. The unfortunate first marquis of Argyll, Archibald Campbell, lies here, beheaded by the newly restored Charles II in 1661.

The Argyll Forest Park reaches the Holy Loch. It was developed during the 1930s by the acquisition of a number of estates. Now, in this part of Scotland alone, the Forestry Commission controls 166,000 acres/67,196 hectares of commercial plantations, mixed woodlands and specialised schemes. The Arboretum above Kilmun has been planted with trees from all around the world. A network of footpaths provides access to many unusual specimens.

On the south side of the Holy Loch, rounded but irregular hills rise from the sandy beaches. Topping them all is Bishop's Seat (1,650 ft/504 m). Opposite, the north shore climbs from the snout of Strone Point to a long rampart of heather-clad, pine-planted hills. The panorama from Cnoc a Mhadaidh (Wolf Hill) (1,542 ft/470 m), takes in sea and sky, island and mountain, and miles and miles of Clyde coastline.

Hunter's Quay

Originally known as *Camasreinach* ('Bay of Ferns'), Hunter's Quay was founded in 1816 by James Hunter, a wealthy merchant. Hunter's Jacobean style mansion, designed by David Hamilton, is now a fine hotel. The quay was added in 1828, rebuilt in 1958, and is one of the last serving piers on the Clyde. Western Ferries use Hunter's Quay as their Cowal point of embarkation.

A typical Clyde villa community developed over the years, centred round the pier and the Royal Marine Hotel. In 1856 the hotel became the headquarters of the Royal Yacht Club. In yachting terms, only the sailing activity around Cork pre-dates that on the Clyde. Swingeing import and export tariffs of the early Georgian period led to a sudden rise in 'recreational' sailing.

The advantages of these boats were quite simple – they were small, quiet, fast and manoeuvrable; and after dark, impossible to trace. As fast as rum and brandy were coming in, whisky was on the way out. It was a busy time, especially for the Excise Men. Occasionally the Gaugers would get lucky. One night two local men were seized, in possession of a couple of casks of contraband, and taken ashore under escort. Somehow, during the rest of that night, the contents of both casks were replaced by seawater and the prisoners had to be released through lack of evidence!

High society came sailing into Hunter's Quay – and royalty, too. A telegraph office was set up so that these important people could keep in touch with the outside world.

The first clubhouse burned down. The new building of 1881 is a prominent feature, commanding a corner of the Holy Loch.

I

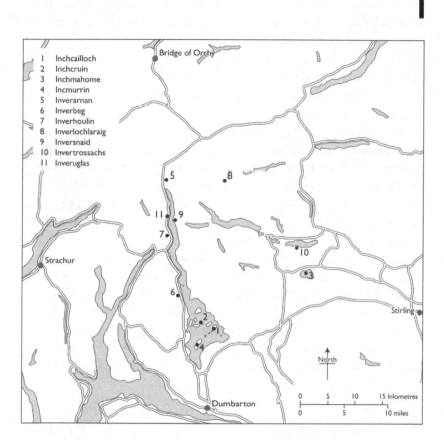

1 Inchcailloch
2 Inchcruin
3 Inchmahome
4 Incmurrin
5 Inverarnan
6 Inverbeg
7 Inverhoulin
8 Inverlochlaraig
9 Inversnaid
10 Invertrossachs
11 Inveruglas

Inchcailloch

Almost touching the mainland at Balmaha, Inchcailloch is Loch Lomond's most accessible island. Early in the eighth century, Kentigerna, daughter of the king of Leinster, settled with the nuns, already well established on the island, and spread the Gospel along east Loch Lomondside. Her influence on the area is still remembered by the name of the old church at Inversnaid. St Kentigerna died on 7 January 734.

'The Island of the Nuns' is veiled with oaks and crowned at its summit by dark Scots pines. The trees hide many of the secrets of this sacred place and the holy women who once lived here. The island was a place of worship until 1670, when the church on Inchcailloch was abandoned in favour of a new building on the mainland. The cemetery remained in use until 1947 and many interesting stones are to be seen.

Inchcailloch is owned by Scottish Natural Heritage but managed by the National Park Ranger Service. The public are actively encouraged to visit the island and the busy ferry unloads many passengers from Balmaha. The high viewpoint is called Tom na Nigheanan, 'Hill of Young Women', and has the most breathtaking 360 degrees panorama around this miniature world. At a mere 279 ft/85 m, it is well worth the climb.

Under the oak canopy, wildlife is abundant. The great woodrush carpets most of the ground. In the summer bats share the trees with a host of songbirds, while timid deer lurk below in the shadows. If you happen to get a glimpse of a pure white hind, it is probably the spirit of a Celtic princess, slain during the Viking incursion of 1263. At a more recent time of strife, World War II, a RAF Spitfire crash landed at this holy place, and the pilot miraculously survived.

Inchmahome

'The Island of St Colm', another name for Columba, is the largest of three on the Lake of Menteith – Scotland's only lake. There was a church on Inchmahome long before Walter Comyn, Earl of Menteith, established his priory in 1238.The prior was a powerful man who not only supported his laird, but also took an active part in the government of the day. This was the ecclesiastical centre for the whole of Lennox.

By the end of the 13th century, the local faerie folk were proving to be quite troublesome, frequently upsetting the human population. So, in 1298, the abbot of Inchmahome used his great authority and banished them. The whole area between Stirling and Aberfoyle became a faerie-free zone. The earl, however, was not too pleased. The faeries had been building him a causeway across the lake to the island, clearly visible today, and the job was not finished.

In 1547, the time of the Rough Wooing, Henry VIII sent an army into Scotland to snatch the queen, five year old Mary. The Scots certainly had dynastic union in mind – but not with England. Stirling was considered unsafe, so Mary spent a few weeks on Inchmahome as a guest of the monks. The queen and her four young companions, all called Mary, built a chapel, designed and established a garden, and planted an orchard. If only they had taken refuge in Edinburgh – they might have built a parliament!

Today the roofless building and ancient stones stand as a silent testimony to Scotland's long, rich and often turbulent history. In the care of Historic Scotland, the priory can be visited by ferry during the summer months.

Inchmurrin

The Isle of St Mirin is the largest island on Loch Lomond and one of three with a permanent population. A mile and a half long from end to end, the highest point is 290 ft/89 m above the loch. Mirin was a 7th century Irish missionary, who may well have lived on the island, and is buried in Paisley. Inchmurrin is sometimes known as the island of hospitality – a reputation enhanced by the availability of the islanders' own whisky.

The castle ruins, at the south west extremity, once provided hospitality for the powerful Earls of Lennox. Not only was Bruce sheltered on Inchmurrin by the 5th earl, but here Isabella, daughter of the 8th Lennox, escaped the full fury of James I – her father, husband and two sons perished at the axeman's hands in 1425. Later, in happier days, James VI hunted over the island before going off to claim his English throne. Inchmurrin was maintained as a hunting reserve until the Duke of Montrose sold the island in 1930.

The early monks, followers of St Mirin, provided shelter and hospitality to all who visited the island. Later, certain women, who had need of 'temporary seclusion', would find themselves reluctant guests on Inchmurrin. The present owner continues to offer hospitality, running a small hotel and restaurant during the tourist season – but they are closed every Tuesday. They run a ferry to Arden, on the west bank, and there is a regular mailboat service from Balmaha.

The best way to explore Inchmurrin is to climb steeply through the birch trees and giant oaks to the top of the open, grassy ridge. Be sure to allow plenty of time to linger and enjoy the magnificent views.

Inchcruin

Inchcruin has had many spellings over the years, such as 'Yniscruny'. Found in Welsh as *ynys* and in Gaelic as both *innis* and *inch*, the word can mean an island, a riverside or a choice grazing for animals. In Latin it turns up as *insula*. *Cruin(n)* translates as round, gathered – as in a group of people – or short, scant or lacking. The Brythonic Celtic form is *crwn* and Old Celtic uses *krundi*.

Through looking at the older names we can have some idea of history and past practices. Low and well wooded, the island is part of a striking archipelago to the south and east of Luss. From time immemorial these island retreats would have been put to good use by the people from the mainland. The Gaelic phrase *chan eil e cruinn*, 'he is not sane', is a clue to an earlier role of Inchcruin. Old records show that this island had been used to confine people with mental problems.

Once part of Montrose Estates, Inchcruin was farmed well into the 19th century, the arable land having been drained and improved by the unfortunate patients. During the last war a little crofting took place on the island; it also became a haven for a large number of films brought out of Glasgow for safe keeping. The last resident, however, seems to have been a lorry.

Inchcruin is half a mile from end to end and has a number of beaches, particularly on the east side facing Milarrochy. The waters to the south are renowned for both salmon and sea trout. There are three known crannogs around Inchcruin, and many fine boulders, giving an insight into the local geology. The mail boat service from Balmaha calls at the island, but only when the old farmhouse is occupied.

Inverarnan

The 17th century Inverarnan Hotel, better known as the Drover's Inn, stands alongside the A82, the Great West Road to the Highlands. This is the bottom of the Laraig Arnan – meaning 'the Pass Through the Alders'. Alder is called *arn* in Scots and *fearna* in Gaelic – the *f* being silent. Countless cattle would have been driven down through Glen Falloch, still dripping with atmosphere.

The drovers and other travellers would have marvelled at the Falls of Beinglas – either spread fine like a Shetland shawl, or raging in full torrent over the dark rock face. The present hotel is an enlargement of the original inn, and was recently modernised to 21st century standards. Many old features have been retained, including the hay cart at the front door. It was put there to stop people staggering out onto the busy road.

There is actually a canal between Inverarnan and Loch Lomond. In 1848, the River Falloch was dredged and straightened from Ardlui, deep enough to accommodate the latest passenger boats. Paddle steamer *Waterwitch* was the first to arrive at Inverarnan, and the basin cut in which these ships turned is still visible. The single stone pillars on either side of the canal were to have carried a 19th century bridge, an idea very firmly vetoed by the Duke of Argyll.

Traffic pours through Inverarnan in greater numbers than the cattle ever did. Between the Drover's Inn and the quaintly named Stagger Inn, there is plenty of refreshment for present day travellers. A bridge crosses the river at Beinglas Farm, allowing West Highland Way walkers to reach these essential services. The farm also has a campsite, with wonderful views of the surrounding hills and the magnificent waterfall.

Inverbeg

Halfway up west Loch Lomondside, Inverbeg, meaning 'Small River Mouth', benefited from an ancient Scots law. It stated that 'There shall be an inn on both banks of every ferry crossing in the land.' Now the ferry to Rowardennan only sails during the summer season. The Highland cattle would have been swum across the loch at this point, greatly shortening the drove to Falkirk and avoiding the toll bridge at Balloch.

Next to the small hotel is the Inverbeg Art Gallery, run for many years by Tom and Kate Merrett. In the custom built gallery you can peruse a large selection of original paintings. The gallery is open every day. From the hotel there is an underpass, allowing access to the lochside without having to dice with the traffic on the A82. A small road slips away to the west, climbing up into Glen Douglas.

The dark, turbulent waters from Glen Douglas flow into Loch Lomond through a delta, built by the river over aeons. It was in Glen Douglas, high above Inverbeg, that the mighty Arthur met and defeated Guillamurius of Ireland, as the Irish came to assist their Scots brethren against the British people. But this was only a temporary setback to the inexorable progress of the new invaders.

The alluvial delta, 500 yards long, provides a perfect timeline to the history of this area. From the caravans standing on the most recent deposits at the mouth of the Dark Water (Dubh Glas), it is possible to walk back to a burial cairn built by our earliest ancestors. Offshore lies one of the smallest islands on the loch – Eilean Deargannan, 'the Purple Island'.

Inverhoulin

A neat, whitewashed coffee shop, restaurant and weaving shed stand a little back from the road, a mile or so north of Tarbet, on the busy A82. Inverhoulin means mouth of the Honeysuckle Burn. The heavy traffic can best be avoided by walking from Tarbet, along a section of the old military road, built by the soldiers from Inversnaid barracks. The track can be found running through the woodland, close to the railway line.

Next to the little coffee shop, Sandy MacPherson is often to be found working at his loom. There is a long tradition of weaving in the Highlands of Scotland, although knitting is comparatively new – introduced by returning Crusaders. At Inverhoulin there are many woven and knitted items for sale, skilfully produced by hand. Scotland, from ten native breeds of sheep, grows a wider range of wool than any other country in the world.

Inverhoulin is covered with trees and overshadowed by Cruach Tairbeirt. The only views are out across the narrow strip of Loch Lomond, to the RSPB reserve at Inversnaid. Tarbet Isle catches the eye, quite small but covered with very large pine trees. In the summer months colonies of noisy gulls take up residence.

Inverlochlaraig

Here, at the head of Balquhidder, was the last of the many houses occupied by Rob Roy MacGregor during his turbulent lifetime. It was here that the old outlaw, pardoned in 1725, passed away peacefully in his own bed, at the age of 74. The original building is still inhabited, standing close to the more recent farmhouse. The high hills are just as Rob would have remembered them.

The small car park at Inverlochlaraig ('the Mouth of the Pass to the Loch') is just beyond Loch Doine. At the end of a long, single-track road from Kingshouse, this is a Mecca for walkers and climbers alike. A good farm road follows the River Laraig west towards distant Glen Falloch. Turn south through one bealach or another and find Loch Katrine, and Rob's birthplace at Glengyle.

A northern route will take you through the hills to Crianlarich and Glen Dochart. The tops of the Munro twins, Stob Binnien (3,822 ft/1,165 m) and Ben More (3,852 ft/1,174 m), can be clearly seen head and shoulders above the rest of the peaks. There are five other Munros within reach of Inverlochlaraig, enough to keep any hillwalker happy.

The history of Inverlochlaraig goes back far beyond the times of the clans. Here Robert Bruce fought a desperate rearguard action, until rescued by local people. Beinn Chabhair (3,061 ft/933 m), at the head of the glen, is said to mean 'Hill of Assistance'. St Angus brought 6th century enlightenment to the iron working Celts and, recently, a Bronze Age site has been identified. Inverlochlaraig is much, much more than just a well run sheep farm.

Inversnaid

Isolated at the north east corner of Loch Lomond, the name means 'Mouth of the Needle (*snàthad*) Burn'. Viewed from across the loch, especially after rain, the spectacular waterfall looks exactly like a needle. At the foot of a glaciated hanging valley, surrounded by oak-clad hills, Inversnaid looks over the water to a magnificent group of hills – the Arrocher Alps, topped by Beinn Ime, the Butter Mountain, at 3,316 ft/1,011 m.

A fort to suppress Clan Gregor was built in 1713.The outlines of Rob Roy's own house can be found behind the tiny primary school, the stone having been removed and incorporated into the garrison walls opposite. A cemetery is to be seen at the back of the school, containing the graves of the non-commissioned officers and men who died at Inversnaid.

The single-track c68 road ends at Loch Lomond, in the car park of the greatly enlarged Inversnaid Hotel, linking with the West Highland Way. From the sheltered harbour, a passenger ferry crosses to Inveruglas, at the mouth of the Dark Water. There is a daily postbus service from Aberfoyle.

Sumptuous accommodation is available at the Duke of Montrose's former hunting lodge, now run as a photography centre. Many weary walkers pamper themselves a bit – a reward for reaching the halfway point of the West Highland Way. Further up the steep hill, the former Church of St Kentigerna has been converted into a comfortable bunkhouse.

Inversnaid is famous for its feral goats, which graze wild over the RSPB reserve. Ancestors of these animals once saved Robert Bruce from capture and certain death, and were rewarded with a Royal Charter, granting them grazing rights at Inversnaid for evermore.

Invertrossachs

Nestling on the south shore of Loch Venachar, tucked in below Loch Drunkie, Invertrossachs has wonderful views of the hills opposite. Formerly known as Drunkie House, the name was changed in October 1859 – at the time Queen Victoria and Prince Albert came to stay. It was thought that Her Majesty would not be amused to be lodged in a Drunkie House, so Invertrossachs it became.

The first forestry plantation to overlook Invertrossachs was spectacularly set out in the battle lines of Waterloo. The owner, a Mr Hunter, was a wealthy draper who supplied uniforms to the army. Subsequent Forestry Commission planting has completely obliterated the plan – something Napoleon failed to do. There are, however, plans to restore the original design.

Invertrossachs House is an Edwardian shooting lodge, set in a tranquil woodland estate. Now being run as Invertrossachs Country House, guests are offered a very high standard of accommodation, with walking, wildlife, boating and fishing all close at hand. There are many other activities within easy driving distance. But, really, who would want to go anywhere else?

There are so many footpaths that any walker would be spoiled for choice. The more adventurous could take the track into Brig o' Turk and gain access to Glen Finglas. Less strenuous, but equally rewarding, is a route up onto the Menteith Hills. For those who like masses of trees, it is possible to walk along and enjoy the facilities of the Forestry Commission Forest Drive. You could, of course, just sit and do nothing at all.

Inveruglas

On an alphabetical list, Inveruglas is the fourth 'Inver-' on the west bank of Loch Lomond. *Inbhir* is Gaelic for a river mouth, and *dhu glas* means dark water. Inveruglas is dominated by the first large hydroelectric scheme to be constructed after World War II, the four massive pipes clearly exposed on the mountainside. Visitors are sometimes told that this is a porridge factory!

Amongst the alders crowded together on a small island, lying low and flat against the estuary, William Wallace took refuge in 1297. A little to the north, and further offshore, the tall dark pines of Inveruglas Isle conceal the remains of MacFarlane's Castle, pounded into ruins by Cromwell's men. The MacFarlanes were an irascible clan, conducting many raids and forays, usually by the light of the moon – MacFarlane's Lantern.

Inveruglas is bounded to the south by the ubiquitous lochside Holiday Park, with caravans and lodges. On the north side is a large parking area and small visitor centre. Hill walkers and climbers heading for adventures in the Arrochar Alps start from here. There is a passenger ferry across Loch Lomond to Inversnaid and the West Highland Way. Overlooking the loch is a viewpoint, to help you get your bearings.

There are many good Inveruglas stories. On a dark night, about fifty years ago, a honeymoon couple were making their way north for a caravan tour of the Highlands. The young woman was asleep in the caravan, dreaming of things to come. At Inveruglas, the husband took a short break. Unfortunately, he drove off again just as his wife, clad in the shortest negligee, stepped outside. Desperately, she flagged down the next set of headlights – a pair of bikers. You can imagine the unsuspecting husband's reaction when, a couple of miles later, the bikes roared past carrying his nearly naked bride!

J

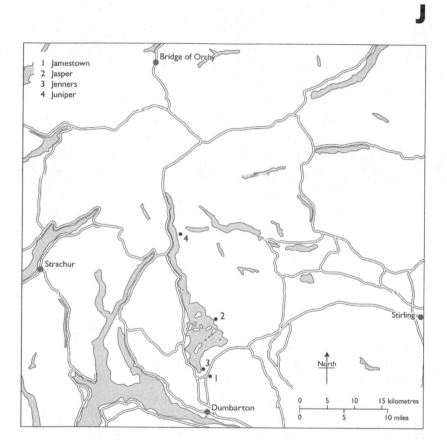

1 Jamestown
2 Jasper
3 Jenners
4 Juniper

Jacobites

'Jacobite' is the Latin word for a supporter of James – James VII, the Old Pretender. In the early 18th century, the lands to the north of Loch Lomond were a hotbed of Jacobite insurgency, led by the MacGregors of Glengyle. The Highland clans were faithful adherents to the Stewart cause, whilst Lowlanders seemed to favour the new order. The anti-Jacobite Duke of Argyll was busy arming the people of Lennox, both to defend themselves and, perhaps, to launch a few attacks of their own.

Rob Roy realised that as soon as he led his men to the uprising, their clan lands would be vulnerable to any foe that could sail on Loch Lomond. So, on 29 September 1715, 70 MacGregors quietly gathered on Inchmurrin. Then, after dark, they sallied out on a raid, the likes unknown since Viking times. Rob's men pulled away along both shores, retrieving every variety of boat that would float, and slipped silently back into the night. Not a single sound vessel was left behind.

Returning to Inchmurrin, sometimes referred to as the Isle of Hospitality, the MacGregors feasted freely on the Duke of Montrose's fine venison and supped plenty of the local whisky – hospitality indeed! At first light, to the relief of the whole country-side, the flotilla rowed away north, towards Inversnaid.

Throughout the 18th century, Jacobite clans rose time and time again, in what turned out to be futile attempts to restore the Stewart dynasty to the British throne.

Jamestown

Sometime towards the end of the 18th century, all the householders of a place called Damhead were named James – so Jamestown it became. Later, Jamestown was greatly enlarged by Archibald Orr-Ewing, who built terraced housing for his growing workforce. Jamestown primary school opened in 1863, the oldest school in the Vale. A parish church was built next to the school in 1869, both constructed from local red sandstone.

Jamestown is the first of the Vale Towns between Loch Lomond and Dumbarton, half a mile south of Balloch. It was here, in 84 AD, at the first fording point of the River Leven, that the Romans encountered a serious problem – the Attacotti. These Attacotti were head-hunters and cannibals and the surviving legionnaires quickly departed.

Flax was widely grown, and with a steady flow of clean, lime free water, linen production was underway along the Leven bank by 1728. At first it was a slow process, needing eight months to bleach cloth naturally in the open air. In 1749 acid bleaching cut the time in half, reducing costs and increasing production.

Cotton imports began to arrive from across the Atlantic; 62,000 kg in 1735, 8.5 million kg in 1861. Woven cotton cloth was sent to the Vale to be bleached, dyed and printed – the Industrial Revolution had arrived.

The dam that held back the water for the Mill of Haldane, and gave its name to a small collection of houses at Damhead, has only recently been cleared. The site is now a petrol station. Much of Jamestown's industrial past has gone, replaced by modern houses.

Jasper

At Milarrochy, on the east side of Loch Lomond, there is a fine exposure of silicified rock, known as serpentine, clearly visible on the roadside – when the loch level is low, it can be seen snaking its way into the water. There are many red and green silica pebbles to be picked up on the beach. This is solidified lava forced into the bedrock some 400 million years ago. Massive earth movements and a great deal of erosion have exposed this formation.

Jasper is the semi-precious stone extracted from serpentine formations. It is a form of quartz, an opaque silica, commonly red owing to iron oxide particles. Green jasper is sometimes mistakenly referred to as jade. Both banded and interwoven red and yellow jasper take a fine polish and can be used for jewellery, buttons and other ornamentation. An excellent specimen from the Campsie Fells was set into the ceremonial baton that carried the queen's message to the 1986 Edinburgh Commonwealth Games.

The burns of the Campsie Fells, especially above Strathblane and Balagan, are a good source of jasper. After especially heavy and prolonged rainfall, lepidopterists scour the burns in the hope of finding a few good, decorative stones. Jasper and banded jasper, commonly referred to as agate, are believed by many to have great healing powers. Not only do these stones have restorative properties, but they have been held, from times long past, to enhance courage – and to build fire in the loins.

Jenners

The ultra modern development at Lomond Shores belies the fact that Jenners is the oldest department stores in the world. The story begins in 1837, immediately after the Musselburgh Autumn Races. Two young drapers, Charles Jenner and Charles Kennington, were dismissed for attending the meet rather than their place of employment. With a single mind, they decided to open their own store, and set about making the ladies of Edinburgh the very best dressed in the world.

Jenner and Kennington secured the lease of 47 Princes Street at an annual rent of £150 and, on 1 May 1838, opened for business. There was a rapid expansion along Princes Street, up South St David Street, into Rose Street, and four storeys skywards. After the death of Kennington, the store was renamed Charles Jenner and Co. In 1873 James Kennedy, who had joined the company as an apprentice, was made a partner. Five generations on, in 2005, this family sold out to House of Fraser.

A month before Christmas 1892, a great fire destroyed the building. Although Charles Jenner never saw his store reopen, he left £8,000 towards the exterior decoration. This included caryatides – female figures carved into columns – to show how women were the support of his business. The first Royal Warrant was bestowed in 1911 and patronage has continued into the 21st century. The Queen made an official visit in 1988, to celebrate 150 years of business.

In September 2002, Jenners opened their outlet at Loch Lomond Shores – their first store outside the original building.

Juniper

High above Loch Lomond, immediately north of the Inversnaid Hotel, is Eurach ('the Place of Juniper'), a juniper-clad hillside. Highland juniper is a small dense plant, more like a bush than the tree that it really is. The Gael will refer to juniper as *euair* – mountain yew – and, like the true yew, it is not actually a conifer; it does not produce cones, but flowers and berries. As the Ice Age retreated and the glaciers melted away, juniper was the first tree to colonise the bleak tundra landscape.

Global warming has pushed juniper into a natural decline – man has made his inevitable impact. Also, domestic livestock, particularly sheep, browse away in all but the most inaccessible places. The berries, when they can be found, take a full three years to mature and are harvested to flavour raw white spirit – gin, which is a shortened form of *genever,* the Dutch for juniper. In the Highlands juniper wood is much favoured by the unlicensed distiller – it burns with great heat and absolutely no smoke.

A number of clans, including the Murrays of Atholl, used juniper as their emblem. Concoctions containing juniper can be used to treat stomach problems, rheumatism and epilepsy. The tree itself will provide protection against many dangers of this and other worlds. The burning of juniper, especially at Hallowe'en, is sure to keep away any unwanted spirits.

This piece of open hillside comes under the management of the RSPB Inversnaid Reserve. There are no sheep on the ground, so the surviving plants only have to tolerate being picked at by passing deer or the odd feral goat.

K

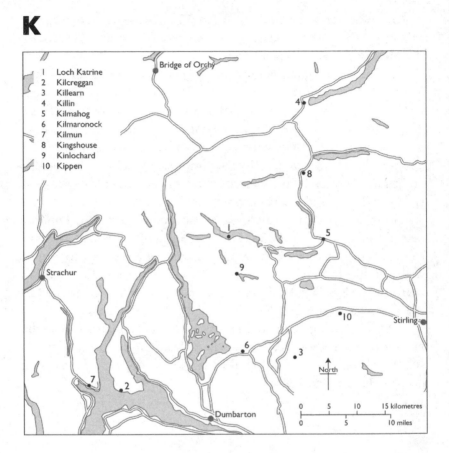

1   Loch Katrine
2   Kilcreggan
3   Killearn
4   Killin
5   Kilmahog
6   Kilmaronock
7   Kilmun
8   Kingshouse
9   Kinlochard
10 Kippen

Loch Katrine

Loch Katrine, from *ceathairne* – a cateran or robber – is undoubtedly the jewel of the Trossachs. It is also Glasgow's main water supply, delivering up to 100 million gallons/500 million litres of water every day to the city. The name Glasgow can be translated as 'the Place of Pure Water', yet, by the middle of the 19th century, cholera and typhoid had become endemic. Pure Highland water soon alleviated the problems, and for 150 years, Glasgow has been able to live up to its name.

Sir Walter Scott frequented the area in search of story lines and background material. His inspirational poem 'The Lady of the Lake' (1812) certainly exposed Loch Katrine to the gaze of the outside world. The beautiful steamship ss *Sir Walter Scott,* launched in 1900, plies the loch under his name. Smaller fishing boats are available for hire and these sparkling waters hold magnificent brown trout and some gigantic pike.

The quiet, 13 mile north shore road is closed to normal traffic. Only Water Board vehicles, people on business and the postbus service from Aberfoyle are allowed access. This always ensures that pedestrians, cyclists and horse riders are comparatively safe and can fully enjoy the serenity. There are storyboards at intervals, to help unfold some of the history and point out features of interest.

Keep a lookout for the Tarbh, pronounced *tarve,* a mysterious water bull. For most of the year the Tarbh lives in the depths of the loch, not bothering man or beast. But after a long, cold and rather lonely winter, he gets a bit hungry and yearns for some company. So, each springtime, he wanders over the hillsides, happily feeding on the wild vegetation and looking for herds of local cows. Any calves born with distinctive ears, like they have been cropped, are known to have been sired by this supernatural bull.

Kilcreggan

Kilcreggan is at the southern extremity of the Rosneath peninsula overlooking the waters of Loch Long, the Gare Loch and the Clyde. The name means 'Church of the Little Rocks', from *cill* – a church – *creag* – a rock – and *an*, a diminutive suffix. Long before any road was constructed, Kilcreggan, a tiny cluster of cottages, was linked to the outside world by ferry.

Following the start of the Clyde steamer services, the growth of Kilcreggan was spectacular. The shore road was built up during the 1880s, with later house built behind on the rising ground. At the top of Donaldson Brae stands the magnificent mansion designed

for the wealthy shipping magnate of that name. It is now the luxurious Kilcreggan Hotel.

Kilcreggan Pier, with ferry connections to Helensburgh and
Gourock, is one of the last working piers on the north side of the
Clyde estuary. PS *Waverley*, the only ocean going paddle steamer left
in the world, calls at Kilcreggan during her summer sailing season.
There is also an hourly bus service to Helensburgh.

There are a number of interesting shops, and a coffee house with
wonderful home baking. A large, strangely painted rock on the shoreline may vaguely resemble a treasure from Tutankhamun's tomb. But
the Tut-Tut Rock was simply the place where bands of itinerant
house painters, brought in to freshen up the villas of Kilcreggan,
would clean off their brushes at the end of the day.

Killearn

The name has certainly changed through history. Kynerine in 1250,
Kyllarn in 1275, Killern in 1430, to the present Killearn. *Earn* is
either a pre-Celtic form of river or refers to St Ciaran, the C having
been lost somewhere along the line. *Kyn* is an alternative for *ceann*
– a head – while *kill* or *cill* can be a church or a division of land.
Given a wide choice, I go for 'the Church of Ciaran', who was a
contemporary of Columba in his Irish days. Ciaran died young and
never left his native land.

Evidence of a long history can be found in other local names.
The Old Celtic *Ibert*, meaning a place of sacrifice, and two 14th
century *Spittal*s, denote further sites of early religious significance.
There have been finds of Bronze and Iron Age artefacts and bits
and pieces from the Roman period.

The present parish church stands where cattle sales took place
until 1860. That most famous MacGregor often did business here,
and once fought a fierce duel with MacNeil of Barra. Sometimes
he needed to take refuge in Rob Roy's Hole, a den down in the
Machar Glen. Such was the life of an 18th century outlaw! The
Black Bull Inn is a living testament to those wild droving days.

A great deal of flax and woollen weaving took place in Killearn. The Old Mill of 1776 becoming a hostelry in 1980. A number of the 18th and 19th century houses have been carefully conserved and are still occupied today. Killearn is dominated by a 103 ft/32 m gritstone obelisk, a memorial to George Buchanan, scholar and tutor to the young James VI.

Killin

Killin is derived from Gaelic *cilltean* – a burying place. Maybe some of the ancient warriors of Finn McCoul – and perhaps even the bones of Finn himself – lie here. Certainly 15 chiefs of Macnab sleep eternally on Inchbuie, their island cemetery below the Falls of Dochart. This village developed round the first stone bridge, built here in 1760.

At the extreme west end of Loch Tay, Killin long remained in isolation – a centre of folklore, myth and legend. A superb little museum, housed in an old mill, tells many of these old tales – stories of witchcraft, early Christianity and strange prophecies. The most remarkable of seers was Baintighearna Labhuir – the Lady of Lawers.

There was also a blacksmith who used a silver sixpence to shoot a woman who dabbled in the black arts. Then there was St Fillan, whose seven sacred relics were each entrusted into the care of a Dewar. A *deoradh* would have been a pilgrim, one who would travel round with his charge. The lands of the Dewar who famously carried St Fillan's 'Glowing Arm' at the Battle of Bannockburn are still called Croit na Mayne – 'Croft of the Hand'.

Then we have the Macnabs. Macnabs are descended from a 9th century abbot of St Fillans – *mac an abba* is 'the son of the abbot'. In 1828, when the Macnab lands fell to the voracious Clan Campbell, a terrible storm blew up. A branch was torn off a pine growing on the Macnab graveyard, and grafted itself on to a neighbouring tree – fulfilling one of the prophecies of the Lady of Lawers. When the lands were restored to Archibald Macnab in 1948, the graft suddenly failed – yes, another of her predictions!

Killin is an ideal centre for golf, fishing, walking and watching wildlife. Every summer there are Highland Games and a festival of folk music... and then there are stories.

Kilmahog

Kilmahog can be translated in three parts, from *cill* – church – *mo* – of my – *Chug* – a personal name, anglicised to Cook. Kilmahog sits at one of only four entrances into the Highlands and consequently has been of great strategic importance throughout history. On the Highland side, behind Eas Gobhain ('Water of the Blacksmith'), stands the ancient bulwark of Dunmore. Below was a Roman fort, built as a natural block on this Highland exit. Roman legionnaires have been heard marching at night, their orders still shouted out in Latin.

A peaceful picnic site nestles comfortably between the two strongholds, within easy walking distance of Samson's Putting Stone. This is a substantial boulder thrown onto the hillside by a local giant, renamed Samson in good biblical fashion. For the less energetic, there are the comforts of the Lade Inn. The food is good, there is often live music and their own beer is brewed on the premises; what more could a body ask for?

Alongside the busy A84 Trunk Road, just before it disappears into the Pass of Leny, there are not one but two woollen mill shops. One has a double advantage over the other; a working weaving shed and the guest appearance of the most famous living Highlander – Hamish Denovan MacKye. Hamish is an enormous Highland bullock with a horn span well in excess of two metres, flowing golden locks, and a very gentle nature. He is actually an exhibit from the Stirling Smith Art Gallery and Museum. This one is definitely far too heavy to hang on their wall.

Kilmaronock

Kilmaronock was part of the great earldom of Lennox, from the Gaelic *leamhonach* – covered in elms. Now it is the parish at the south east corner of Loch Lomond. The name Kimaronock translates as 'the Church of Ronan', identified as being the Bishop of Kilmaronen, in Lennox, at the time of Bede. A plain church stands alongside the A811. The building dates from 1873, but inside there is a list of the incumbents since 1325.

From the Celtic Earls of Lennox came the MacFarlanes. Parlan was the son of the Malduin who stood shoulder to shoulder with Bruce at the Field of Bannockburn. The Celtic earls soon gave way to the new, powerful Anglo-Norman aristocracy. The royal house of Stewarts claimed the Lennox for themselves. Through the marriage of Lennox daughters, Kilmaronock came first to the Flemings, then to the Dennistouns and finally to the Cunninghams, Earls of Glencairn. When Glencairn sold the estate in 1667, he brought to an end 338 years of family control.

It was the Dennistouns who built the castle at Kilmaronock, probably late in the 14th century. It is a rectangular keep, four storeys high and, although quite ruinous, largely intact. Entrance was gained at the second floor level, having been reached by an external wooden stair – quickly removed when the need arose. The family coat of arms is incised in the stone above the door. Similar in structure to castles at Culcreuch (Fintry) and Duntreath (Strathblane), such fortified towers were unique to Scotland.

Kilmun

The name Kilmun was recorded as early as 1240 and refers to St Fintan Mannu, a companion of St Columba. Nothing exists of this early Christian settlement, and only a stone tower remains of the second church, built in 1442. This collegiate church was built by Sir Duncan Campbell, over the grave of his son Celestine. This son of the Black Knight had died in the south and attempts to return his body through Lamont territory for burial at Loch Awe had been thwarted by deep snow and winter storms. Lamont willingly granted his neighbour services of grave and flagstone.

Many great Campbells were to follow Celestine into the mausoleum. Later the Campbells, in inimitable fashion, butchered the Lamonts and seized their lands.

David Napier, the great marine engineer, built a pier at Kilmun in 1827. A hotel and six identical houses, known as the Tea Caddies, soon followed in a speculative venture. Napier put a road through to Loch Eck and, by a series of steam coaches and steam ships, it was possible to travel in some comfort to and from Inverary, on Loch Fyne.

The Age of Steam, largely pioneered by Napier, brought prosperity to the Clyde coast. Kilmun became an attractive village of south-facing villas. The present snecked-rubble church dates from 1841 and has some notable stained glass windows and a water-powered organ. The cemetery has an ancient hog-backed grave and many old, tradecraft stones, the oldest being of a tailor buried in 1697. Elizabeth Blackwell, the first woman doctor, is laid to rest there, too. Two heavy, cast iron mortsafes are in place to deter passing bodysnatchers.

Kingshouse

The long narrow pass, taking the A84 into the Highlands, suddenly opens out at Kingshouse. All at once there are magnificent views over wide meadows and deep into the Balquhidder glen. This Kingshouse, along with others, was established as a base for the soldiers building military roads, under a policy to subdue the Jacobite clans. The plan to pacify the Highlands was that of General Wade. This section of the Stirling-Fort William road was actually built by Caufeild's men in 1757.

The earliest date of settlement at Kingshouse is 1571. Here, from earliest times, weary and hungry travellers would have found hospitality of sorts. Redcoated troops were certainly billeted at Kingshouse in 1747 – and for many years after. On 1 March 1779, a lengthy petition on behalf of drovers was presented to the Commissioners of Forfeited Estates, asking for a new Kingshouse to be built. The cost was set at £40.

The black and white hotel, situated just off the main road, still serves fine ales and has an extensive menu utilising fresh local produce. The bar has an interesting array of old weapons and a welcoming open fire. It is an ideal place to break your journey, or to explore the surrounding area. Kingshouse is on National Cycle Route 7 and the Rob Roy Way, a 77 mile trek between Drymen and Pitlochry.

Kinlochard

Kinlochard, revered in song and legend, is buried deep within the Loch Ard Forest. In English, it is 'the Head of the High Lake'. The sheer beauty of the area brings in visitors from all over the world, and has done for many years. Some of them never go home. The very last English giants, Gog and Magog, lie sleeping on the south shore of the loch, sheltered by trees. The Devil himself came too, until the local Wise Women chased him away. Demonic footprints can still be seen in the exposed rock alongside the River Forth.

Mile upon mile of newer tracks have been made by the Forestry Commission, now harvesting 68,000 tonnes of timber a year. The forestry roads are ideal for people out to enjoy a gentle walk or for those making their way to the higher ground. It is not unknown to encounter a team of huskies harnessed to a wheeled rig.

The Park Authority has implemented a limit on all powered boats using Loch Ard. Officially designated a quiet loch, a wide range of safe water activities have been developed by the Sailing Club and at the Watersports Centre. For those who must make a noise, quad biking, 4x4 safaris and clay pigeon shooting are all available at Kinlochard.

Forest Hills is a 25 acre, landscaped complex of hotel, time-share apartments and leisure club. It is open to the public and there are two restaurants to choose from. This is the place for curling, either to watch or play – the quality of the ice is superb. Just stay for a while and enjoy a drink or a meal.

Kinlochard is not only in the Highlands of Scotland, it is at the heart of the first National Park. All this, and only an hour from the centre of Glasgow!

Kippen

From two words with the same meaning: Scots Gaelic *caep* – headland – and Brythonic *pen* – head or end. To the south, precipitous hills are reputed to have hidden the lair of the last dragon in these parts. To the north, long ago there was nothing but water and bottomless bogs. This was the last bastion of the old kingdom of Strathclyde. No wonder they used to say 'Oot o' the world and in tae Kippen.'

Roman earthworks, along with a motte and a ruined church with an overgrown spring – both dedicated to St Mauvais (died 544) – are evidence of historic settlement. St Mauvais' Fair, 26 October, was one of a series held between March and October. In addition there were special markets on the first three Wednesdays of December. Large numbers of wild Highland cattle would change hands at these trysts, up on Balgair Muir.

It was during the raid on Kippen, in September 1691, that Rob Roy MacGregor lifted the entire Livingstone herd. He also swept all the livestock out of Kippen, just for good measure. The old kirk yard holds the remains of Jean Kay or Wright, a wealthy young widow, carried off and forced into marriage by Rob Roy's youngest son, Robin Og. It all ended unhappily; Jean died of smallpox and Robin Og was hanged for his crime.

In more recent times Kippen has been famed for its gros coleman vine. Planted in 1891, by 1922 it had become the biggest cultivated vine in the world. The Kippen vine avoided pestilence and disease, and even survived the greenhouse being destroyed by the great storm of 1927. In 1964, with a lifetime total of 103,243 bunches of grapes, the vine was cut down. A chess set was carved out of its roots.

L

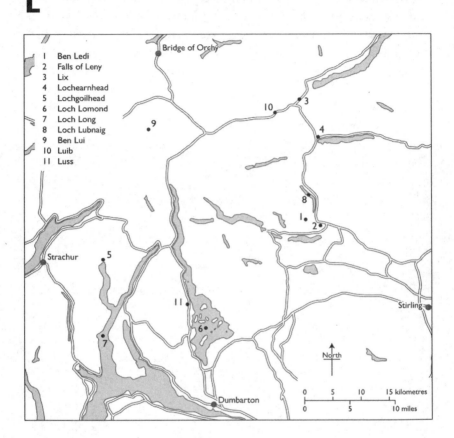

1 Ben Ledi
2 Falls of Leny
3 Lix
4 Lochearnhead
5 Lochgoilhead
6 Loch Lomond
7 Loch Long
8 Loch Lubnaig
9 Ben Lui
10 Luib
11 Luss

Ben Ledi

Ben Ledi, north west of Callander, is a contraction of *ben le dia* – mountain of the god. The god venerated on this shapely 2,875 ft/ 879 m peak, so prominent on the skyline of the southern Highlands, was Bel, the Celtic sun god. The festival of Bel, from *be'uill* – life of all – was called Beltane, 1 May, and was celebrated well into the 20th century. The festival was to ensure enough light and warmth would be provided to nurture the growing crops.

Every fire was extinguished and on Ben Ledi, as the sun touched the sky on May Day morning, a new fire was kindled. The home fires were relit from these pure hilltop flames. Later, as the fire died down, the young people cooked and ate an oatmeal bannock, to which a small piece of charcoal had been added. Whoever found the piece of charcoal had to leap three times over the fire, a stylised form of self-sacrifice. It was hoped that this appeasement of Bel would guarantee a good harvest.

The word Beltane comes from the Gaelic expression, *La Duidhe Bealltuinn*, 'the Yellow Day of Bel's Fire'. On this day too, their cattle were driven between two special fires, to purify and protect these prize possessions. Cows were currency, used in all sorts of payment – known as 'blackmail'. 'Black' just refers to the colour of the animal and *màl* means a rent or money due. Later, thanks to the local MacGregors, blackmail came to relate to any payment made under duress.

Beltane fires no longer burn on Ben Ledi, and people climb to the summit simply to take in the great panoramic view.

Falls of Leny

A mile north of Callander is the Pass of Leny, from *lanaigh* – a wet place – one of four major entries into the Highlands. Over countless ages, the land has been sculpted into its present shape. The Garbh Uisge (Rough Water) slices through the pass, joining Loch Lubnaig to the River Teith. Especially after rain, the twin cataracts of the Falls of Leny are truly awe-inspiring, thundering over hardened volcanic ridges. This damp, tree-shrouded chasm is a visitor's delight and a botanist's dream.

Along this gloomy defile came early man and his many successors, emerging into fertile Strathyre. The Romans marched northwards and black cattle came south. Redcoated soldiers laid a fine military road, still extant in many places. Then came the hard turnpike toll road, annoying the feet of the livestock and the pockets of the drovers, but improving communication across the Highland Line.

The railway, hard-won from nature (and some reluctant landowners) was a remarkable feat of Victorian engineering.

Nature, however, never surrenders. Rocks and boulders rained down onto the railway track and the line had to be walked and cleared on a daily basis. After one large rock fall too many, the railway was abandoned, before Dr Beeching had even lifted his axe. The track is now part of the long-distance Rob Roy Way and National Cycle Route 7. There is ample parking on the north side of the A84, opposite the falls and at the start of a forest walk.

Lix

In two other places in Scotland the name Lix is said to derive from *lic*, locative of *leac* – a place of flagstones. This third Lix, just to the west of Killin, could have a much more interesting origin – the Romans. During the reign of Hadrian, the 9th legion of the Imperial Roman army marched into the Scottish Highlands – and vanished. The fact that this expeditionary force of 6,000 men simply disappeared was of no great consequence; the Romans were used to losing the odd legion. It was the loss of the sacred insignia that caused them some concern. For 30 years after the 9th legion went missing, crack Roman commandoes made lightning raids into the Highlands. In the entire history of the Roman Empire, the Eagle of the 9th was the only one they lost and were unable to recover.

Some say that the men of the 9th legion simply deserted, others believe that they were completely vanquished by local tribes. An alternative view is that the legion was disbanded and merged with other units – much like the fate of our Scottish regiments today. Whatever happened, there are three marks left on a stone near Killin that appear to read 'L IX' – possibly standing for 'Legion Nine'. Perhaps this was a last SOS left by these desperate soldiers in a foreign land.

Our Celtic ancestors left us their marks too. Hidden amongst the trees, very close to the busy A85 and the junction with the

A827, is a classic cup and ring marked stone. This whole area is rich in history.

The Lix Toll filling station is widely known for a selection of unusual Landrovers. One bright yellow vehicle stands a long way off the ground and runs on caterpillar tracks. Lix is seemingly well prepared for heavy snowfall, rising sea levels, and possible meteorite strike!

Lochearnhead

Lochearnhead is an anglicised form of *Kinlochearn* (Head of the Lake of Enchanted Water). *Earn*, some say, also means Irish, from *eireann*. It is worth noting that the local word for a sea eagle was *ern*, and there used to be plenty of these magnificent birds around the loch. The headwater rises above the village and falls 1,800 ft in three miles, into the loch below.

In the frequent wet spells of weather, tributaries around Loch Earn plunge down the hillsides, white, wild and full of spirit – and when the skies clears, they are gone. The narrow loch is six and a half miles long, stands 317 ft/97 m above sea level, and is said to have deeper places than the official 287 ft/87 m marked on the chart. Swimmers should be aware that the loch bed can suddenly drop away, often within a few feet of the shore. Safe and organised activities are run from the Watersports Centre on the north shore.

Lochearnhead stands at the junction of the roads from Stirling (A84) and Perth (A85) to Oban and Fort William, on the west coast. The road northwards leads through stunning Glen Ogle, described by Queen Victoria as Scotland's own Khyber Pass. Her Majesty never visited India; perhaps somebody sent her a postcard of that distant corner of the Empire!

A circular route around Loch Earn makes a pleasant drive, although the unchecked trees obscure much of the view. On the south shore, Highland cattle graze round Edinample Castle. At the roadside is the burial ground of the Campbells of Monzie. Close by are the Falls of Edinample. Here old stories easily blend into the beautiful scenery, and the clan names of Stewart, Macdonald, McLaren, Macnab, MacNeish and MacGregor echo from the hills and across the water.

Lochgoilhead

Spread around the head of the Loch of the Stranger is found one of the most interesting villages of Argyll. If not arriving by sea, you will come via an extremely narrow road, with many passing places – an experience in itself. For the faint hearted, there is a bus service from Helensburgh.

The original settlement took root on the eastern seaboard. Later extensions westward have culminated in extensive chalet development and caravan parks. The medieval Church of the Three Brethren makes reference to a small band of Celtic saints who became established here in the 7th century. The oldest part of the building is from 1379, with many additions and improvements made up to the modernisation carried out in 1955. There is an ancient stone font and a carved stone memorial to the Campbells of Ardkinglas, buried here since the 15th century. Next to the church, in a private garden, stands another Campbell monument dated 1626. This is a carved sandstone sundial, 10 ft tall and thus, for mere mortals, rather impractical as a means of telling the time.

The countryside can be covered by bicycle, on horseback, or on shanks' pony. One of Rob Roy MacGregor's many caves can be explored, as can the tumbling falls of Donish Water. To the west, the summits of Beinn Bheula (2,515 ft/779 m), Beinn Lochain (2,265 ft/697 m) and Beinn Thorsuinn (2,011 ft/619 m) may draw the more adventurous out.

A new radio mast at Lochgoilhead has greatly improved communications. Those who enjoy going out on the water can do so in the knowledge that the coastguard has the Loch Goil area well and truly covered.

Loch Lomond

Loch Lomond has the largest surface area of any fresh water in Britain – 27.45 square miles. The loch is 23 miles long, 5 miles wide at the southern end, and deeper than the North Sea. Loch Lomond takes its name from the great guardian mountain, Ben Lomond – 'the Hill of Fire'. In ancient times warning beacons were often lit on the 3,914 ft/974 m summit. Ben Lomond is the most southerly of the 284 Munros. A well worn path from Rowardennan leads eventually to the trig point, perched on the edge of a sheer drop. The views are second to none; the Lowlands to the south and vast mountains all around.

The loch, so beloved of artists and writer throughout the ages, is famous for three phenomena. There are sometimes waves without wind, caused by a sudden change in atmospheric pressure pushing water up into the narrow northern reaches. Then there are the fish without fins, parasitic lamphrey, one particular species being unique to Loch Lomond. Finally, islands that float! These are rafts of floating peat, sometimes quite large. In the late 16th century, people and livestock actually lived on one.

Loch Lomond has more species of fish than any other loch. Powan are found here; flounders, normally seawater fish, have also been recorded, and some of the biggest ever pike have been taken from these waters.

There are magnificent views from the A82 over the whole length of the loch. However, some of the finest views have become obscured by trees. You can, of course, stop at any of the viewpoints. But the very best way to see this loch, with its 38 islands and garland of mountains, is from a boat out on the beautiful expanse of water.

Loch Long

Loch Long is indeed very long – 17 miles from where Glen Loin runs into the sea at one end, to the Firth of Clyde at the other. The name actually means 'Loch of the Ships'. *Luing* – of the ships –

appears as the name of this loch in an Icelandic Viking Saga. The Norwegians also refer to it as *Skipfjord*, with exactly the same meaning.

In 1263, Haakon of Norway dispatched 60 of his longboats into the waters of Loch Long. A number of these boats were dragged for a mile and a half overland, and then launched into Loch Lomond with devastating effect. From Tarbet, the Vikings set about their business, doing what Vikings were very, very good at doing – burning, pillaging and... you know the rest!

For many years Loch Long was used for testing the torpedoes manufactured for the Royal Navy at Alexandria. Today it is the setting for more peaceful pursuits. The sheltered water, with such clear visibility, attracts many divers.

Loch Long has rich fish stocks: cod, whiting, herring, plaice and mackerel can all be caught, and the autumn brings runs of leaping salmon, as they make their way towards their freshwater breeding grounds.

This is wild and rugged walking country. There is road access to many points along Loch Long – and many more places to which there is not. Section Six of the 47 mile Cowal Way comes in over the hill from Lochgoilhead – the final stretch to Ardgartan. There are good bus links to the head of Loch Long, and it is not too far to the nearest station on the West Highland Line.

Loch Lubnaig

Loch Lubnaig is certainly well named – 'the Loch of the Bend'. The water has been squeezed and twisted along four miles of bonnie Strathyre, a great fissure rent in the Highland Wall. Escarpments on either side block out much of the sky and the sun can only be a transient visitor. Tall, dark conifers deepen the shadows and add to the gloom.

The loch, a 100 ft deep at a point just west of Ardchullarie More, would once have been dotted with crannogs. Each of these

man-made islands was linked to the shore by a cunningly concealed causeway of stepping stones. Crannogs were safe refuges in
times of danger, especially if every boat had been removed from the
shoreline.

Nowadays a couple of lochside car parks give easy access to
the water and lovely beaches. At the south end of Loch Lubnaig
stands the ruined chapel of St Bride, originally known as Bridget,
who lived between 452 and 524 AD. With her new name, St Bride
was used to supplant Brid, the ancient fire god of the Celts – a
change of name and a change of sex!

The early Christians were well aware of the importance of fire to
the people they were trying to convert. At the festival of St Bride, the
Church introduced the Christian Candlemas, keeping the sacred
Celtic element of fire. The crusaders made such a cult out of St
Bride that every crusader's wife became known as his own Bride.

An ancestor of McKinley, President of the United States, sleeps
in the walled ground of St Bride's chapel.

There are many walks available at Loch Lubnaig, along forest
tracks or the old military way. The road across the bridge leads to
a forestry car park and the west side of the loch – and to the climb
through Stank Glen to Ben Ledi.

Ben Lui

Ben Lui means 'Hill of the Calf' (*laoigh*), a place where red deer
hinds will still gather at the end of each May, almost ready to drop
their dappled calves. Clear all-round views enable the herd to slip
quietly away from any approaching danger. This mountain is an
absolute classic, perfectly formed and full of character.

It is no surprise to find that it was on the slopes Ben Lui that
the newly founded Scottish Mountaineering Club pioneered winter
climbing techniques. The precipitous Central Gully was first climbed
in 1891. At 3,707 ft/1,130 m, snow will linger well into the summer months. Even without snow, this is a very special mountain.

Access to Ben Lui is found 1.5 miles south of Tyndrum. Turn west through Dalrigh, where Bruce was defeated by the MacDougalls of Lorne, and trek four miles towards the massive amphitheatre of Coire Gaothaich ('the Windy Gully'). Above Cononish Farm are extensive quarry workings and several abandoned mines – there really is (or was) gold in them thar hills!

Amongst the jumble of scattered rock, the exposed geology is fascinating. You can find ancient schists, limestone – some of it formed into marble – and lumps of volcanic whinstone. Look out, too, for crystals of pink garnet.

The confluence of Allt na Rund, coming from the west, and Allt Coire Laoigh, flowing from the south, has long been recognised as the start of the River Tay. Beyond, Ben Lui looks formidable indeed. There are several climbs to choose from, or you can just stop here and take in the dramatic setting.

Luib

Luib is no more than a neat, whitewashed sixteenth century droving inn, set in the heart of Glen Dochart ('the Glen of Sorrow'). *Lùib* is Gaelic for a bend or a corner and, although the busy A85 has been greatly improved, both the road and the river wiggle their way through the length of the glen. This is a good place to stop for refreshment.

The area is one of outstanding historical interest. Ruins range from tumbled down castles to more humble dwellings, and empty summer shielings are hidden away in the hills. Then there are the strange stones bearing ancient cup and ring marks. A little to the west is an old, walled Macnab graveyard. To the east is an important burial mound, giving its name to the farm, Ledcharrie, from *leud carraigh* – the broad plain of the monument.

The Luib is an excellent base for many activities. Golf, tennis, bowling and a full range of watersports are all within a short drive. Salmon and trout fishing are only a cast from the door of the inn, and deer stalking can be arranged. The traditional stag shooting season runs between 20 August and 20 October.

It is as a centre for hill walking that the Luib comes into its own, with the high Breadalbane hills to the north and the mountains of Balquhidder to the south. From the Luib there is a good six mile walk through the Ledcharrie Glen and over the high pass to the village of Balquhidder. This route, once much favoured by drovers and smugglers, is now only used by ramblers and fishermen. The small loch, hidden in the heart of the pass, is said to contain very unusual trout – white fish with red spots.

Luss

Luss is the Glendarroch of television fame, as featured in the long running Highroad saga, set on the west bank of Loch Lomond. Now a conservation area, Luss is a very beautiful and well kept village. Originally known as Clachan Dubh, because of the dark hill shadows cast by the early sunset, the name eventually changed to Luss.

After her death in France in the 14th century, the body of one Lady MacAuslan, late of Luss, was returned to the lochside, embalmed in herbs and flowers. Some of the fleur-de-lys took root on her grave. These exotic flowers were gathered and used as charms, believed to ward off outbreaks of plague and other illnesses. Whether the new name derived from these lilies or from Gaelic *lios* – garden – it is impossible to tell.

The present church of St Kessog dates from 1875, built as a memorial to Colquhoun of Luss and five of his men, who were drowned in a great storm. A number of churches have stood on this site, going back to the times of Kessog himself, martyred nearby in 520 AD. Many of the ancient gravestones are thought to date back more than a thousand years – the oldest of their kind in Scotland. There is also a richly carved Viking hog-backed stone from the 11th century.

Leave the madding crowds and follow the Luss Water inland, to a quiet, enchanted glade with a natural bathing pool. Further upstream are the ruins of a weaving community, a link with the busy industrial past of this area, which included slate quarrying, iron smelting, gold prospecting, and distilling.

M

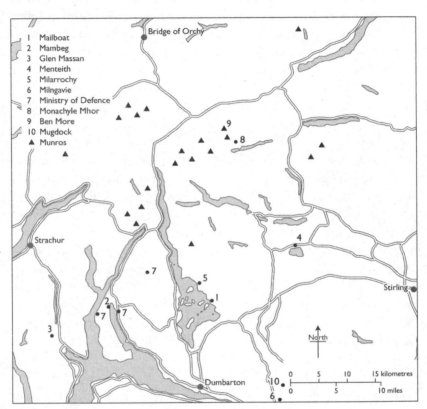

1 Mailboat
2 Mambeg
3 Glen Massan
4 Menteith
5 Milarrochy
6 Milngavie
7 Ministry of Defence
8 Monachyle Mhor
9 Ben More
10 Mugdock
▲ Munros

Mailboat

Since 1948, three generations of MacFarlane have been entrusted with the Royal Mail services on Loch Lomond, sailing out from Balmaha. As fare-paying passengers can also be carried, this is a perfect way to see the loch in all her glory, and get a true perspective of the scale of the mountains. Descended from the Celtic Earls of Lennox, the MacFarlanes have been living on the lochside for centuries. It has even been suggested that Noah called in for tea, as the Ark drifted by at the time of the Great Flood!

Two traditional wooden vessels, both launched about 60 years ago, are in service. *Margaret* is 32 ft, beautifully teak built; *Marian* is 38 ft with a red funnel, very fitting for a mailboat. Summertime services to the three inhabited islands, between May and October, run every Monday, Thursday and Saturday, leaving at 11.30 am. During July and August, it becomes a daily sailing. Winter deliveries are reduced to Monday and Thursday, departing at 10.50 am.

Lunch is provided on the island of Inchmurrin – but not through the winter and never on a Tuesday. However, the Oak Tree, at the entrance to the boatyard, is open all day, all year round, and the food is always excellent. Especially recommended is the Arctic char, a fish only found in a few northern lochs and a relic of our glacial past. Over time, each of these lochs has evolved a quite distinct species of the fish – and they are all absolutely delicious.

Leaving from the lowland side of the chain of wooded islands, marking the line of the Highland Boundary Fault, the mailboat sails northwards into a deep fjord, splitting the mountains for 20 miles. This is a wonderful opportunity to see Scotland at her absolute best.

Mambeg

The Gaelic word *mam* is often used as a colloquial term to describe a rounded hill with gentle slopes, somewhat resembling a human breast. However, *mam* can also mean a lump, boil or ulcerous swelling – even a mole. To this end, many of the hills called Mam were places to which such human afflictions could be transferred, through the power of old Celtic charms. With a neat pair of hills – Mambeg (*beag* – small) and Mamore (*mor* – big) – guarding the way into Rosneath Peninsula, I prefer the first option in this case.

Mambeg is a coastal settlement of eight houses, stretched along the B833, well separated but tightly squeezed between the trees of Garelochhead Forest and the water of the Gare Loch. At low tide there is a long, stony beach, usually covered with a wide variety of flotsam. Mambeg is a geologist's paradise. Clear evidence of the

Highland Boundary Fault can be seen in the well-rounded stones on the shoreline and in the exposed bedrock.

Pier Road at Mambeg ends abruptly at the water's edge; the pier, like so many others, has long gone. Children still come and learn to swim, or play happily in rock pools and turn over stones. Many Royal Navy divers undergo training in these waters and sea anglers come to catch dogfish, for which the Gare Loch is renowned. They are a great delicacy – once you have learned how to skin them.

There is plenty of wildlife to be seen at Mambeg, both in and out of the loch. Seals occasionally pop up, but there are stories, perhaps no more than rumours, of a stranger creature being seen in the water...

Glen Massan

The three highly glaciated glens, Massan, Lean and Eck, drain their waters into the Holy Loch. An unclassified dead end road runs into Glen Massan, north west from the A815, past the exotic golden gates of Benmore Botanic Garden. These magnificent portals came from the Great Exhibition of Glasgow in 1888. The 20 acre garden, run as part of the Royal Botanic Gardens, Edinburgh, is renowned for a collection of over 250 species of rhododendron, and an avenue of redwood trees that greets every visitor.

The mid glen section is quite dramatic. To the right of the road, just south of Stonefield, is a rock outcrop showing superb glacial gouges and grooves. Further up the glen, amongst craggy slopes and fallen rock, a waterfall marks the place where the river is cutting into a deeper bed, still adjusting to the lower level of the Holy Loch. In places the water has left natural arches of stone across the river.

Above the falls and beyond the reach of the last Ice Age, which ended some 10,000 years ago, the river meanders more gently across a much flatter landscape. From the end of the road there is a three mile climb to the top of Beinn Mhor (2,413 ft/741 m), a place where sheep used to be brought for their summer pasture.

Glen Massan is a delightful place. When, after rain, the river is in full spate and the waters plunge over falls and roar through deep cauldrons, it is quite easy to understand why the glen was so revered in ancient Celtic verses.

Menteith

Menteith was one of the earliest divisions of the Celtic kingdom, ruled over by minor kings. By the Middle Ages the earldom and title of Menteith had been invested with considerable political power. But now Menteith has become much diminished, reduced to a small area overlooked by the Menteith Hills, but famed for having the only lake in Scotland.

The name has been derived from *moine* – a moor – and *teith* – a river tributary (in this case, of the Forth). The term 'lake' came into use after 1305. It was John Stewart of Menteith who betrayed William Wallace to the English. The change of name is a fitting memorial to that terrible act of treachery.

The Lake of Menteith covers more than one square mile and has been a managed fishery since the 1920s. Long recognised as the finest rainbow trout water in Scotland, many of the top fishing championships take place here. 12 lb rainbows and 8 lb brownies are not uncommon and, besides the fishermen, heron and osprey compete for the catches.

A summer ferry sails to Inchmahome and the ruined Augustine priory, built in 1238. Five year old Mary Queen of Scots was sheltered here during the Rough Wooing of Henry VIII, who wanted her as a bride for his eldest son, Edward. At that time the Scots had no designs on the English crown – the prospect of a union with France was another matter altogether. The Auld Alliance was very much alive.

On the south side of Inchmahome can be seen the causeway that local faeries were never allowed to complete.

Milarrochy

Milarrochy is tucked away on the east side of Loch Lomond. The road from Drymen passes through Milton of Buchanan and Balmaha, to the car park and boat launching site at Millarochy Bay. The road continues as far as Rowardennan, but no further – unless you are walking. At the north end of the Pass of Balmaha is a fine stretch of golden sand and the Manse Bay car park. If the gate to the field is open and there is somebody to collect the money, there will be a charge for parking.

Half a mile from Manse Bay, along the unclassified road, is Milarrochy. This name is a translation of *meal* – a promontory – and *larachain* – a small ruined farm. The promontory is clearly visible on the left hand side of the road. The ruins of an ancient dun or fortified tower are hidden amongst the trees. Milarrochy has a free car park, free boat launching, and really excellent toilet facilities. During the summer there is a manned information point. The gates, however, are locked at night.

The spectacular pebbled beach is a happy hunting ground for both geologists and lapidaries alike – or anyone else who likes picking up pretty things. Well washed and rounded stones, from both sides of the Highland Boundary Fault, are evident. Signs of Scotland's turbulent past can easily be found in the volcanic rocks and glacial debris that litter the loch shore. The prominent serpentine reefs, snaking out into the water, are an endless source of smooth, red and green specimens. The feel is quite therapeutic.

With the loch, the hills and the fine oak woodland, there is much of interest at Milarrochy. But if it is walking you want, it is south to Milngavie or north to Fort William.

Milngavie

The name Milngavie may come from the Gaelic *Meal na Gaoithe*, meaning 'Hill of the Wind' – but is commonly held to be simply 'Gavin's Mill'. And mills there were aplenty, all powered by the

Allander Water. Some of the old buildings are extant to the present day.

Milngavie, only 10 miles from Glasgow city centre, is a small town in a pleasant setting, with Mugdock Country Park and the Scottish Water reservoir complex just to the north. This is the water from Loch Katrine, en route to the metropolis.

Milngavie has a first class shopping centre, with a new supermarket standing on the site of the old Black Bull Inn. Rob Roy MacGregor frequently traded cattle at the local sales and competed, with some success, in the wrestling tournaments afterwards. It was here that Rob was arrested and imprisoned in Mugdock Castle – he escaped when he found that the door of his cell had been left unlocked!

There are traces of Roman occupation. The Antonine wall passes to the south, built between 139 and 142 AD to keep the northern tribes out of the Empire. Here, too, are the vestiges of George Bennie's wonderful Railplane Project (1930–1937). This luxurious monorail service, powered by aircraft engines, was never extended beyond the 1.5 mile test section, and foundered through lack of investment. There is still a rail link to Glasgow, but it is a bit slower than it might have been.

Milngavie is officially the start, or finish, of the West Highland Way, just 95 miles from Fort William. However, there is now an added link to the Botanic Gardens in the centre of Glasgow.

Ministry of Defence

The Ministry of Defence has control of some 14.5 square miles in the vicinity of the Loch Lomond and Trossachs National Park. Great swathes of land have been fenced off. Behind the barricades, however, are secret wildlife reserves. Together with many other organisations, the MoD has developed management plans to ensure the welfare of these undisturbed habitats.

Faslane submarine base has become home to a large colony of common gulls. There are also eider ducks, first recorded on the Clyde in 1904, now well established and breeding at several sites, particularly in Loch Long. Artificial nesting platforms set up for ospreys are in use, but not by the magnificent fish hunters they were intended for. Buzzards moved in first, only to be evicted by the much smaller kestrels – such is nature. Snow buntings descend from Scandinavia and take up winter residence on the grenade range, bursting through the air like feathered shrapnel. The birds seem to be quite unaffected by the activities of military man.

A tree regeneration programme has been to the benefit of black and red grouse, and to the turkey sized capercailzie. Mammals too have prospered, and roe deer numbers are now quite high. It is hoped that the increase in tree cover will enable red squirrels to make their way south from their present stronghold at Arrochar.

Organised visits can be arranged with the Wildlife Liaison Officer, based at Coulport. But next time you are driving through Glen Douglas, along Loch Long or past Faslane, look beyond the chain-link and razor wire. With a current bird count of 110 species, including the graceful hen harrier and the ballistic peregrine falcon, there is a very good chance of seeing something special.

Monachyle Mhor

On the north side of the Braes of Balquhidder, overlooking deep Loch Doine, stands Meall Monachyle (2,110 ft/648 m). Gazing west from Balquhidder, at Monachyle the mountains seem to close in and almost touch across the glen. Monachyle comes from *monadh* – a mountain – and *caol* – a narrow place. Another source gives *moine* – a moor – and *coille* – a wood. Trees there are aplenty, but there is hardly room enough for a moor.

A good many years ago, in a way typical of many West Perthshire hill farms, much of Monachyle Glen was sold off to the Forestry Commission. Still, the best part of 1,000 hardy, blackface sheep graze over the remaining pasture, up upon the hill. Each ewe will keep to her own ground, giving birth to her lambs within a few feet of where she was born. There is also a herd of 50 suckler cows, producing the finest Scotch beef.

At the 18th century farmhouse things are a little bit unusual. The pale, pink-washed Monachyle Mhor is one of the finest restaurants in Scotland. This has to be farm diversification at its very best! The views are stunning, the food is outstanding, especially the beef... and to save having to drive home after a night out, there is accommodation too.

There are lochs to fish, scenes to paint and a sun to watch, as it rises over one Ben Vorlich and, at the end of the day, goes down behind another. Monachyle Mhor is an excellent base for hill walking. There are a number of fairly level walks, some more ambitious routes up into the Highland glens and passes, and six Corbetts and seven Munros at hand for the really adventurous.

Ben More

When it comes to naming geographic features, the Scots show a singular lack of imagination – the land is awash with Black Lakes and festooned with Big Hills. Of all the Ben Mores ('Big Hills') in Scotland, this well known landmark standing to the east of Crianlarich is the highest, at 3,851 ft/1,174 m. The symmetrical cone, clearly visible from all points of the compass, enhances the impression of great height – especially when capped in winter snows.

Many years ago, while climbing Ben More, the early members of the Scottish Mountaineering Club quickly came to realise that Scottish mountains required the same respect as the high Alps. Ben More covers six square miles of steep, wild and trackless country, whose ever changing moods can mean danger for the ill-prepared and unwary.

Access is usually from the A85 to the north, with ample parking at Benmore Lodge and Loch Iubhair. The normal approach follows the steep climb from Benmore Farm. For a while you will be staring into the bowels of Benmore Glen. Soon the views will begin to open out and, from the hard-won rocky summit, half of Scotland lies before you. Whether you will be able to see any of it is quite another matter.

For the more adventurous – those who have made proper transport arrangements – descent can be via Stob Binnein (3,822 ft/1,165 m) and down the Inverlochlarig Glen. Alternatively, you could cross to Am Mam and go south to the comforts of Monachyle Mhor, on the Braes of Balquhidder. Always my first choice!

Mugdock

The reservoirs at Mugdock were constructed by Victorian engineers to collect and distribute daily 100 million gallons (500 million litres) of fresh and pure Loch Katrine water. For more than a century, this untreated supply was acknowledged to be the very best water in the world. Now it has to be rigorously and expensively treated to meet European standards! The landscaped grounds of the complex were gifted to the people of Glasgow to enjoy forever. But now they have been extensively fenced by order of the Special Branch.

The name Mugdock was first recorded in 1372, when the Earl of Lennox transferred the barony and castle to David de Grahame. It could well refer to the rent of one merk – a silver coin worth 13.5 pence – paid for a measure of land – a *dabhach*. The ancient south tower of the castle has been well preserved and there are also traces of the old chapel. Once protected by Mugdock Loch, the water level has been reduced, leaving the ruins standing high and dry and open to all.

At Mugdock Country Park there are 640 acres/260 hectares of woods and moorland to explore, castles and lochs to discover, and a garden centre to enjoy. Open every day, there is a visitor centre, tearoom and designated recreational area. There are many ranger led activities and a full and varied programme of events.

There are trains to Milngavie and a bus service to Mugdock. The first section of the West Highland Way goes through the park – and for those who must drive and come by car, there is ample parking.

A
Aberfoyle
Claims to be 'The Enchanted Village'.

B
Balquhidder
Burial place of Rob Roy MacGregor.

D
Duck Bay

This lively marina was once one of Scotland's top night spots.

E
Ellen's Isle

Largest island on Loch Katrine which is home to moles, though nobody knows how they got there!

F
Forestry

200,000 tonnes of timber are removed each year from the National Park's forests.

H
Highland Boundary Fault

This massive geographical marker was formed 450 million years ago.

J
Jenners

The store at Loch Lomond Shores is the first branch outside of the famous Princes Street store.

L
Falls of Leny

One of four major entries into the Highlands.

M

Mailboat

Since 1948, three generations of MacFarlane have been entrusted with the Royal Mail services on Loch Lomond.

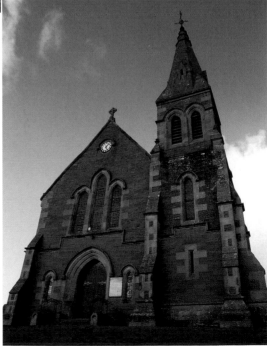

N

Norrieston

A secret route for cattle once passed through this village.

O
Oak

Oak trees in the area hid sacred groves where priests conjured up their spells.

P
Peace Camp

The Faslane sit-in, which began as a temporary measure in June 1982, has now lasted more than 20 years.

R
Rest and be Thankful

Many a traveller have taken their ease here on the 900ft / 274m summit.

T
Teapot

The Wise Women of Strathard (local witches) used to live near the Teapot Cottage.

W
West Highland Way

The 95-mile walk from Milngavie to Fort William was officially opened in 1980.

Y
Yachting

Loch Ard yachting club currently boasts a double Olympic Gold medallist.

Munros

There are 21 Munros – mountains over 3,000 ft – in Loch Lomond and The Trossachs National Park, and another good half dozen close by. Ben More, at 3,851 ft/1,174 m, is the highest. In 1891, Sir Hugh T. Munro published his list of 283 summits, each one separated from adjacent peaks by a minimum descent of 100 ft. The list has been much revised, but since 1997, stands at 284. Munroists set out to 'bag' them all.

In 1996, an agreement was reached between all vested interests – the Concordat on Access to Scotland's Hills and Mountains. This actively encouraged reasonable and responsible access, and set out to ensure due consideration for all parties using the Scottish Uplands. Many rural economies derive much of their income from shooting, stalking and sheep farming. Without their stewardship the landscape would change beyond recognition.

The 2004 Countryside Access legislation has further widened and clarified the situation, enshrining in law what most Scots saw as common right. It is worth remembering that with these rights come an awful lot of responsibilities. The countryside is not just a playground.

Our mountains provide a home for people as well as for wildlife. They yield pure and life giving waters, supply produce for the table, and offer a refuge from the stresses of the 21st century.

Unfortunately there are a number of accidents, sometimes fatal. The arctic flora, thriving on the upper mountain slopes, should be a warning sign. Even in the height of summer, winter conditions can strike. Be adequately dressed, properly shod, and always leave word of your route.

N

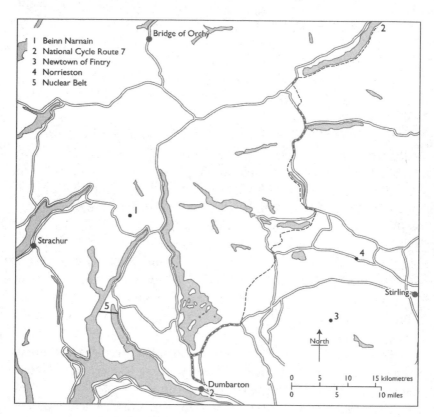

1 Beinn Narnain
2 National Cycle Route 7
3 Newtown of Fintry
4 Norrieston
5 Nuclear Belt

Bridge of Orchy

Strachur

Stirling

Dumbarton

North

| 0 | 5 | 10 | 15 kilometres |
| 0 | | 5 | 10 miles |

Beinn Narnain

Beinn Narnain is often referred to as the Cobbler's Left Hand Mountain, a true Munro at 3,038 ft/926 m. The origin of the name is shrouded in mystery, though there are three possible explanations. There is an ancient Celtic word for water, *nar* or *naro*, still found in places around the Mediterranean. Certainly, from the summit of Beinn Narnain, if it is not shrouded in mist, a great deal of water can be seen. In 1895, the journal of the Scottish Mountaineering Club came up with Varnan, from *bhear nan* – the notches or gaps at the eastern cliffs, known as Spearhead Rock. But I like the legend that speaks of the giant called Narnain who lies slumbering, still clutching his spear, and whose name lives on in this mountain form.

Access to Beinn Narnain is usually from Succoth Farm, where Glen Loin runs into Loch Long. There is car parking alongside the A83 and, for those who would rather not drive, a bus service from Helensburgh. A path into Glen Loin leads steeply through the trees, and eventually to the open hillside. Follow the line of concrete blocks, remnants of the railway used to build the Loch Sloy hydroelectric scheme. The fading path leads through rocks to the Spearhead. Climb a gully on the right hand side, up to the stony plateau.

Serious hill walkers set off for Beinn Narnain with every intention of going on to even bigger and higher things. Beinn Ime is only a short distance to the north west, just across the Bealach a'Mhaim, and a snip at 3,316 ft/1,011 m! The total ascent over the seven mile round trip is reckoned, by Cameron McNeish, to be 4,000 ft/1,219 m, for which you should allow seven hours.

National Cycle Route 7

National Cycle Route 7 is part of a well designed, 10,000 mile cycle network covering Great Britain and Northern Ireland. It is possible to cycle in comparative safety from Land's End to John o' Groats. Pedestrians can take full advantage of these paths, and much of the network is suitable for disabled and wheelchair access. A 60 mile section of National Cycle Route 7 crosses Loch Lomond and The Trossachs National Park.

The route meanders in from the south, along the banks of the River Leven, to Loch Lomond at Balloch. For the next 30 miles the cycle route turns east by north and teasingly traces the line of the Highland Boundary Fault. The Pass of Leny, just north of Callander, is the entrance to the real Highlands, a mountain fastness of lochs, glens and breathtaking scenery. Before leaving the area along Loch Tayside, National Cycle Route 7 has passed through more than 30 places of interest covered in this A-Z series.

Working in partnership with local authorities and many land-owners, Sustrans (it stands for Sustainable Transport) continues to expand the network. A new bridge over the River Forth will complete the Aberfoyle to Buchlyvie link along the line of the old railway. By utilising such obsolete tracks, tow-paths and riverbanks, one third of the network is expected to be completely traffic free. National Cycle Routes will not only provide safe human passage, but will also become wildlife corridors into the very hearts of our towns and cities.

National Park

It was John Muir, the great pioneering Scottish environmentalist, who helped to establish the world's first National Parks – Yellowstone and Yosemite – in the USA. Other countries followed suit. England and Wales took up the idea in 1949, but Scotland was left lagging far behind. After years of talking, Scotland finally emerged in the new century with a National Park in place – almost.

In its very first year, the Scottish Parliament passed the National Parks (Scotland) Act, 2000. Plans for Loch Lomond and The Trossachs National Park were drawn up and the opening date set for 19 July 2002. An Interim Committee was put in place to ensure the fully fledged Authority could hit the ground running. Time has passed – the park is here, but many of the concepts of the Interim Committee have not seen the light of day. However, the present Board is able to build on sound foundations.

New Codes of Conduct for Loch Ard, Loch Eck and Loch Earn have already been implemented. A raft of new bye-laws is to be introduced, to deal with a range of longstanding issues. Lack of speed restrictions on Loch Lomond and some strange planning decisions are just two of the issues giving cause for concern. A small but well organised team of rangers and wardens do their best to maintain a number services across 720 square miles of National Park. No mean feat.

The National Park Plan was published in 2005, after public

consultation and much delay. Public involvement is crucial to long-term success. So far, only 25 per cent of the population is in any way involved through the Community Futures scheme – not nearly enough.

Newtown of Fintry

In 1796, Fintry was a village on the move, uprooting from the old clachan where the church and the Clachan Hotel still stand, three quarters of a mile due west of the present site. The Newtown of Fintry is an excellent example of 18th century industrial development, and is still remarkably preserved. The name means 'White House', from the Scots Gaelic *fionn* – white – and the older, Brythonic, *tref* – a house or a homestead.

Early in 1778, Peter Speirs, a wealthy tobacco merchant, bought Culcreuch estate and the 15th century castle, ancient seat of the Clan Galbraith. Fourteen years later Speirs took in hand the existing corn mill and added a new cotton mill to the site. Across the river, on the south side of the Endrick Water, his new houses were rapidly filled. Many of the new mill workers came from Dewsbury, Yorkshire.

In 1901 the estate was sold to Walter Menzies, MP for South Lanarkshire. The new laird quickly made his mark on the Newtown. Where the road from Kippen crosses the 1804 stone bridge, Menzies placed a fine iron fountain to commemorate the coronation of Edward VII. In 1907, to mark the coming of age of his son James, he built and presented a fine new hall to the village. Electricity was connected by underground wires to the castle and many of the houses, generated by the water which once powered the mill.

Fintry was once famous for the annual Daffodil Tea. The young maidens of the village would go and gather armfuls of wild daffodils to decorate the hall. All the eligible men of the district were then invited to tea, while the young innocents strutted their stuff. There are still plenty of daffodils around Fintry.

Norrieston

The 90 ft spire of Norrieston parish church overlooks the settlement named after Robert Norrie, a servant to both James I and James II, who received these lands in 1482. On a raised beach above the northern edge of Flanders Moss, a vast quaking bog, Norrieston was at a natural crossroads. A secret route lay across this dangerous morass, coming north towards the Highlands from the Fords of Frew. Many sleek cattle came this way, never to be seen again.

Westward, along the dry ridge, was an ancient track to the Highland Pass of Aberfoyle. The Romans later came and paved it – as Romans liked to do. The Earl of Lennox passed by on his way to avenge the wanton murder of James III, only to be ambushed on Flanders Moss by James IV, and put to flight. Soldiers would leave Stirling and march through Norrieston on their way to subdue the clans – and would pass through again on their way back, chased home by the savage Highland men. Norrieston was a busy place, and about to become much busier.

In 1695 an act of Parliament permitted a weekly market and four annual fairs. Each of the fairs was to last eight days. Many fiery Highland cattle were traded here, as wild and hairy as the men who drove them. But changes were afoot. Much of the Moss was being drained and brought under cultivation. The fairs were replaced by an agricultural show, and farmers were left to show off their skills at ploughing matches. The biggest change of all was happening right on their doorstep – the new development of Thornhill.

Northern Lights

The Northern Lights are called Aurora Borealis, Latin for 'Dawn of the North'. In fact, Aurora was the Roman goddess of the dawn. The Celts saw the lights as the Heavenly Dancers. These strange lights in the atmosphere, radiating from the region of the Pole, form luminous curtains, bands, arcs and patches in the night sky.

The greenish rays are sometimes tinged red at the edges, and can put on some fantastic shows.

The lights are best observed during the long dark nights of the winter months, but can occur at any time of the year. They appear after a period of intense solar activity caused by sunspots. The raging solar winds energise tiny particles in the oxygen and nitrogen atoms in the upper atmosphere. Look out for the Northern Lights after a couple of really windy days when the atmosphere has been well and truly disturbed.

High energy produces green colour while low energy produces red. The Northern Lights will switch on and off in rapid, almost instant, response to changes in energy levels. The aurora can increase atmospheric nitric oxide and be responsible for a measurable fluctuation in the ozone layer. Some of the nitric oxide will be washed to earth in rainfall, helping to maintain soil fertility. Nitrogen stimulates plant growth.

These Heavenly Dancers have been seen as far south as Madrid, but not very often. Here, on a dark night, under a clear sky and away from light pollution, if you happen to be looking in the right direction, they may dance for you.

Nuclear Belt

Since 1992, Britain has given up all air launched nuclear weapons, all nuclear artillery, and disarmed the nuclear capability of her surface fleet. Now, the nuclear capacity is retained by just four Vanguard class ballistic submarines, located along with the entire nuclear arsenal... on the Clyde estuary, right on the doorstep of Glasgow.

There is always one submarine on patrol, carrying 48 British built warheads. The Trident delivery system is, however, courtesy of Uncle Sam. A total of 58 missiles have been bought from America, and those not at sea are stockpiled at Coulport, on Loch Long. Also at Coulport are nearly 200 warheads, each with eight times the power of the Hiroshima Bomb. The submarines, *Vanguard*,

Victorious, *Vigilant* and *Vengeance* are based at Faslane, in the Gare Loch.

The nuclear warheads are manufactured at Burghfield, near Aldermaston, in Berkshire. Every few months, a large, heavily protected convoy will travel north with a deadly cargo. Although each warhead contains plutonium and other radioactive materials, no radiation symbols are ever displayed on the vehicles. Weapons are also returned to Burghfield for routine servicing. That adds up to a lot of dangerous freight on the move.

Earlier generations of nuclear submarines are already being decommissioned. Over the next 30 years as many as 27 of these vessels will be dismantled, and all the radioactive components stored at Coulport – on a temporary basis, so they say.

The nuclear stockpile has been reduced by a third and each weapon load is down by half. But what is left is stored 40 miles from the centre of the biggest city in Scotland.

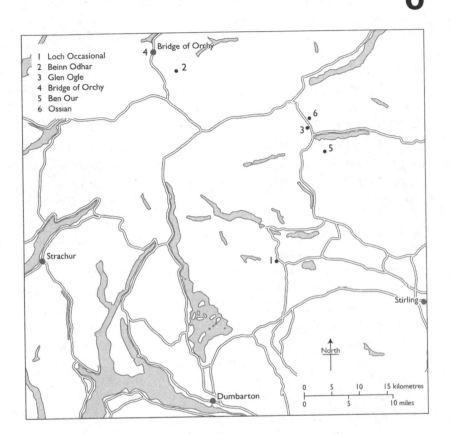

1 Loch Occasional
2 Beinn Odhar
3 Glen Ogle
4 Bridge of Orchy
5 Ben Our
6 Ossian

Oaks

The oak is known in the Highlands as darroch, from the Gaelic *dhariach*. This tree outlives all others in the forest except the yew, often living more than 700 years. It is frequently struck by lightning and sometimes bears mistletoe, both the very essence of the Celtic gods. The oak was believed to hold power, strength and energy from both heaven and earth.

Priests conjured up their ancient spells in sacred groves, hidden by the oaks. Kings held their power through the tree, oak leaves worn on the royal head and a sceptre of oak held in the royal hand. Their courts were held beneath the spread of oak branches. Charles II even found shelter in one, after the battle of Worcester in 1651.

The oak lined straths and glens in this area are remnants of 17th century plantations. Coppiced on a 24 year cycle, every part of a felled tree was used – the bark to tan hides and the wood for charcoal (used to smelt iron, added to many patent medicines, and an ingredient of gunpowder). Oaks grown through two cycles provided wood for house building. Trees reaching 72 years of age produced timber of ship building quality. Any waste wood was distilled into pyroligneous acid, used for setting the dyes in the local textile industry. The introduction of a new generation of chemicals during the 1920s brought coppicing to an end and now the oaks grow on, quite untroubled by man.

As many as 284 other forms of life can be found on an oak, each tree a nature reserve in its own right. No other tree carries as many species – horse chestnut has five, plane tree only one and rhododendron none at all. High rainfall ensures that liverworts, lichens, mosses and ferns can live upon the oak. Insects infest oak flowers, inhabit the bark and eat the leaves. Spiders stretch webs to catch their prey. Small birds nest and feed on the insects. Many of these small birds become food for larger birds and animals. All over the oak something is eating something else.

Leaves and acorns fall to enrich the soil, feeding a host of other organisms and nurturing a carpet of wild forest flowers. If the oak is not harvested for timber, ivy, mistletoe and fungus will begin the slow process of decay. In the space left by a departed tree, an acorn is sure to grow.

Loch Occasional

Water is one of the major resources of Loch Lomond and The Trossachs National Park. It falls in copious amounts, sometimes causing a degree of flooding. At Aberfoyle, under certain conditions,

Loch Occasional will appear. There are several interesting facets to this loch, not least the speed with which it arrives and departs.

The warm, moisture laden Atlantic air stream rises steeply over the Scottish mountains, condensing into the rain clouds that always keep the Highland lochs well topped up. After a typical West Coast deluge, the water cascading off the shoulders of Ben Lomond and pouring into Gleann Dubh will meet the River Forth, a mile west of Aberfoyle. If this coincides with the time of the high tide on the east coast, there is nowhere for the water to go. Although more than 25 miles from the sea, Aberfoyle is only 82 ft/25 m above sea level, and so the rainwater pools here.

As the water spreads into the surrounding fields, there is a distinct possibility of the school being cut off and the children being dismissed. The road to Strathard and the communities of Stronachlachar and Inversnaid can soon be lost underwater and the village car park is often completely awash. If Loch Occasional continues to rise, sandbags begin to appear at vulnerable points and the adventurous take to the streets in their boats. Once the tide turns, the water level rapidly falls and Loch Occasional simply disappears – until next time.

Each year nine billion tonnes of water fall upon Scotland – from which we manage to produce 2 million gallons/9 million litres of whisky. Not a bad exchange rate!

Beinn Odhar

This is 'the Dun Coloured Hill'; one of many of this name. When it comes to naming features of their landscape, the Gaels often choose the patently obvious. The country has many features with similar sounding names. However, some names can have several different meanings – that is just Gaelic! So, Beinn Odhar may also mean 'the Dappled Hill' – which is much more picturesque.

Beinn Odhar (2,955 ft/901 m) stands astride the northern point of the National Park boundary, overlooking the Bridge of Orchy. This is the start of the only group of Corbetts with five tops, a considerable undertaking if attempted in one expedition. From the West Highland Way, cross under the West Highland Line and ascend the steep slopes of the south west ridge, making use of an old mining track. As the gradient eases a small lochan appears, said to be the haunt of the faeries and much deeper than it looks.

From the summit cairn the views are quite outstanding, surrounded by Corbetts and Munros. The five top traverse will drop down the south east side, to another wee lochan, draining into the Allt Choire Dhuibh. This is en route for Beinn Chaorach (2,685 ft/818 m) – Sheep Hill. Local poet Duncan Ban MacIntyre hated the sheep that had cleared so many people from the land. His 'Song of the Foxes' exclaims, 'My blessings upon the foxes, because they hunt the sheep!' Below, in the Auch Gleann, the poet's old house is being used as a sheep fank!

The summer sunrise will cast the shadow of Ben Ledi onto Stuc Odhar, while between Callander and Glen Gartney stand Meall Odhar, Tom Odhar and another Beinn Odhar – all meaning Dun Coloured Hill (or maybe not).

Glen Ogle

According to Queen Victoria, Empress of India, this is Scotland's Khyber Pass. Glen Ogle may be on a much smaller scale than the Himalaya, but to any cyclist who has ever peddled uphill into a rain lashed gale, it is quite big enough! It is a three mile pull through a 600 ft/188 m climb. The name Ogle comes from *ogluidh* – gloomy, awful or terrible. Other names on the landscape here are clues to a turbulent history: Was it at Lix that the Roman 9th legion left their last mark? From what fate did Ossian deliver the local people, to have a hill named Creag na h-Oisinn?

Creag na Tollair tells a story still well remembered. In 1610, a new Act against the persecuted Clan Gregor made their heads worth collecting. Gregor MacGregor, the clan chief, was being pursued by the Earl of Argyll's specially trained bloodhounds. As the belling hounds reached the top of the pass, the chief shot and killed the leading animal at Creag na Tollair ('the Rock of the Hound'), ending the chase. Well, for that day, anyway.

The old railway track, clinging to the rocky slopes, is now part of National Cycle Route 7. At the head of the glen, the cycle path links to the Glen Ogle Trail, a popular walk from Lochearnhead. Good footwear is recommended.

At the foot of the glen are a few very old houses, just standing back from the road. Although quite dilapidated, some of them still have original turf and thatch roofing. They look a bit draughty now, but people occupied these humble dwellings not so long ago.

Bridge of Orchy

Orchy got its bridge in 1751, as Major Caulfeild pushed through his military road from Tyndrum to Kinlochleven. The name Orchy refers either to the colour or actual presence of gold in the water, washed out of the bedrock by the turbulent river. Glen Orchy is the largest parish in Argyllshire, but only the straths of Lochy, Strae and Orchy are habitable, along with the shoreline of Loch Awe. The rest is untamed mountain.

Orchy was renowned for an ancient forest of great Scots pines. In the 1820s, at a price of 6d (2.5p) each, the trees were felled. Monarchs and their nobles frequently hunted through the forest in pursuit of deer, boar and fugitive MacGregors. When James VI, in faraway London, heard word of a white hind in Glen Orchy, he sent for her to be brought to Windsor Great Park – to be within the king's range.

After the road came the railway, in 1894; the West Highland Line. Although there are excellent bus services through Bridge of Orchy, the best way to travel is by train. The railway sweeps round the base of Beinn Odhar, over a viaduct, and doubles back under mighty Beinn Dorain (3,530 ft/1,076 m). This majestic mountain has never been better praised than by the words of Duncan Ban MacIntyre, born here in 1724. This unschooled stalker and poet captured the very essence of Beinn Dorain in a word cycle of 550 lines.

With seven Munros and seven Corbetts close at hand, this is true mountaineering country. And there is always the Bridge of Orchy Hotel to return to, where you could add a small drop of the golden river to a wee dram of golden spirit.

Ben Our

Marked on the Ordnance Survey map as Ben Our (2,405 ft/733 m), it is also known as Ben Or, 'Hill of Gold'. This name may well come from the colour of the high pasture, as the molinia grass takes on its summer hue. It could also be a reference to the gold held within the mountain – the reason for the Roman invasion of 79 AD; mineral wealth. Ben Our, rising at the south west corner of the loch, is a clear landmark the whole length of Loch Earn and beyond. The starting point for Ben Our is a small lay-by just beyond Edinample Castle, at one time the home to the Marquis of Breadalbane. By the roadside is a Campbell burial ground. If you are parking, please do so carefully; the south shore road is very narrow. A farm road leads off into Glen Ample and the Ample Burn tumbles over the falls, towards the loch. Turn left at the farm, otherwise you will find yourself heading for Meall nan Oighreag ('the Hill of the Cloudberries').

Beyond the farm, a footpath continues between the burn and a deer fence until a bridge crosses the river. Straight on at this point would take you to the route through to Loch Lubnaig, so bear left for Ben Our. Picking up a hill road, there is a stiff climb through the inevitable plantation but, once clear of the trees, you are well on the way to the top. The views begin to open up. Below can be seen Glen Ample, while all around are brooding mountains with precipitous, dark crags.

The road suddenly comes to an end. Just keep climbing. Look out for signs of old summer shielings, where long ago domestic livestock grazed away the long summer days. Look too for both the Scotch argus and mountain ringlet butterflies – exclusive to these upland areas. And Ben Our has one other surprise – not one summit, but two!

Ossian

Ossian was one of the sons of Finn McCoul, a giant warrior chief who lived in the 5th century. Finn spent a great deal of time in West Perthshire, building 12 castles in Glen Lyon alone. Well, it is Scotland's longest glen. Ossian took all the adventures of his father's people, the battles they fought and the hunts they enjoyed, and put them into story form. These tales have been passed down through countless generations, many still being told today. A traditional greeting is, *Bheil dad agad air na Fionn?* – Do you know any tales of the Finn?

One story is told of how Ossian got his own wife. She came to him one dark and stormy night in the body of a crow. Through Ossian's great kindness to her the spell was broken and she resumed human shape. She promised to live as his wife until such time as he referred to her previous form. Many happy years passed before that fateful slip, and in a flurry of black feathers, she was gone, leaving only a gold ring behind. But this was the ring of immortality and for as long as Ossian wore the ring, he would never die.

For three centuries Ossian wandered these lands, telling his stories. Tales of how the stars of the Plough were placed in the sky by his father; of why the tears of his own daughter turned the heather white; and many, many more. Creag na h-Oisinn in Glen Ogle commemorates the story of how Ossian saved the people there from a terrible fate. Since the time when the ring was separated from Ossian's finger, he has slept under a large boulder in the Sma' Glen of the Highlands.

P

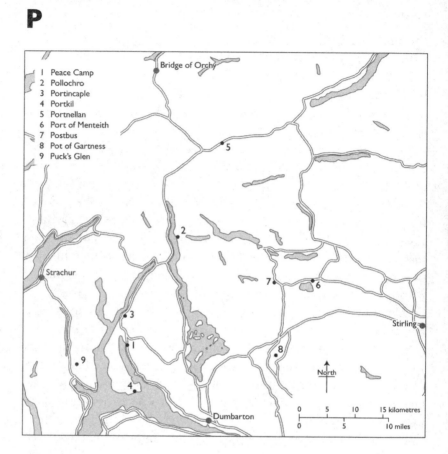

1 Peace Camp
2 Pollochro
3 Portincaple
4 Portkil
5 Portnellan
6 Port of Menteith
7 Postbus
8 Pot of Gartness
9 Puck's Glen

Bridge of Orchy

Strachur

Stirling

Dumbarton

North

0   5   10   15 kilometres
0   5   10 miles

Peace Camp

The peace camp, set up opposite HM Naval Base Clyde, began as a temporary measure on 12 June 1982. With the proliferation of ever more destructive weapons looming on the horizon, the anti-nuclear campaign was rapidly gaining momentum. Apart from endless debate and countless columns of newsprint, protests took the form of marches, demonstrations and sit-ins. The Faslane sit-in has lasted more than 20 years.

Naval activity in the Gareloch intensified during World War II, with submarines operating from floating depot ships. The modern base at Faslane Bay has at its origins the arrival of the 3rd Submarine Squadron in 1958. Following an agreement with America, that Britain was to be supplied with Polaris Nuclear Missiles, the 10th Submarine Squadron arrived in 1967.

Originally established on MoD land, the camp soon moved along the A814 to the roadside village of Shandon. The former Strathclyde Council and Dunbartonshire District Council were sympathetic to the Campers, the local authority charging only a nominal rent of £1.00 per month. However the present council of Argyll and Bute is less supportive, the courts granting them a right of eviction.

The peace camp at Faslane is well run, with strict rules and a code of conduct to be observed both on and off site. Wood burning stoves provide heat for warmth, hot water and cooking. Electricity is produced by bicycle generator. Many flowers and shrubs have been planted, including a cutting taken from a special cherry tree; one that survived the Hiroshima blast. The cutting was planted by two Japanese ladies, who also survived that nuclear holocaust, which killed over 75,000 people.

Police

The policing of the Loch Lomond and Trossachs National Park is a massive undertaking. The park covers 720 square miles, has almost 400 miles of road and a population of 16,000 people, plus six million summer visitors. Five separate police forces have responsibility in and around the National Park, Central, Strathclyde, Tayside, Ministry of Defence, and British Transport.

There is a great deal of liaison between these authorities, frequently involving Mountain Rescue, Coastguard and Customs & Excise. National Park and Forestry Commission Rangers are given advice on how to deal with the often serious problems they face. The rangers depend on police backup for much of their operation

– though it is not always readily available. Central Scotland Police are currently recruiting 100 new officers to improve this situation.

Apart from their role in maintaining law and order, the police are involved in framing any bye-laws the National Park may wish to introduce. Working with the wider community, the police have already set up the Crime and Disorder Partnership, an inter-agency organisation looking at a wide range of issues.

Dealing with wildlife crime is now recognised as a priority. The Loch Lomond and Trossachs National Park has 57 designated sites under the Wildlife and Countryside Act, 1981. Close cooperation between so many bodies is coordinated by Sergeant John Simpson (MoD, Coulport), Wildlife Police Officer of the Year in 2004.

Pollochro

Three miles good walking north of Inversnaid is Pollochro, a derelict farm. Long abandoned, the ruins are only visited by feral goats – famously given protection by Robert Bruce – and West Highland Way walkers. The name comes from *poll* – an embankment – *achadh* – a cultivated area – and *reidh* – flat; a good place to farm.

The surrounding woodland, fringing east Loch Lomond, is mostly oak, mixed with alder, ash, birch, rowan, holly, hawthorn and hazel. Other trees include apple, aspen, bird cherry, blackthorn, elder, juniper and yew – and a fine stand of old sycamores at Pollochro. In springtime the woodland floor is carpeted with flowers – over 650 species have been identified. Every April, the resident bird population is swollen by a wealth of summer visitors. Pollochro is now one of the largest RSPB reserves.

A steamship was built here about 1840, using the plentiful oak timber. The *Waterwitch* transported lumber to the Clyde, returning with cargoes of coal and other goods. After plying her trade for many years, the *Waterwitch* was sold, refitted, and taken to the high seas. This ship, built at Pollochro, sailed around the world.

There are ferry sevices across Loch Lomond from Ardlui and Inveruglas, linking with the West Highland Way. There is also a daily postbus from Aberfoyle to Inversnaid. From Inveruglas or Inversnaid, the only way to get to Pollochro is to walk. This is one of the last true wildernesses, a haven for most wildlife. It is a great pity that the RSPB continue to shoot King Robert's goats.

Portincaple

On the east side of Loch Long, Portincaple may translate as 'Port of the Chapel', from *caibeal*. More likely it is derived from *capall*, a horse, so 'Harbour of the Horse'. Portincaple was a very busy place indeed. A drove road followed the high ridge south from Arrocher, and is still visible in places. Although it was no great distance by land, many cattle were swum across Loch Long to avoid the hazards of MacFarlane country. The marinated animals came ashore at Portincaple.

Fishing, and later tourism, underpinned the local economy. Although there was no pier at Portincaple, steamer passengers were landed by small boat, as part of a tour of the Three Lochs. The promised railway station at Portincaple never materialised, but the one at Whistlefield was close at hand. Trains still run on the West Highland Line, but Whistefield station is long closed. There is a Monday-Friday bus service from Portincaple to Garelochhead, which has to be booked by telephone 24 hours in advance.

Portincaple is a scattered community of mostly single dwellings surrounded by woodland and rampant rhododendrons. The vista across Loch Long is absolutely stunning. The rocky shore is festooned with mussels, and the dark rock highlighted by veins of white quartz, bright yellow lichen and delicate sea-pink flowers. Often there will be a smell of wild mint, crushed underfoot.

It is no wonder that people here guard their privacy. There are prohibition signs everywhere – Private, No Admittance and Keep Out. Finding a way to the beach is not easy. Thankfully, there is one sign that boldly declares that walkers are welcome.

Portkil

On the north shore of the Firth of Clyde, Portkil means 'Port of the Monastery'. There was a strong and early Christian influence on the Isle of Rosneath. Until recently isolated at the southern tip of the peninsula, the only communication with the outside world was made by boat. Now there is an hourly bus service from Helensburgh.

A thatched farmhouse stood for many years at Portkil; a cruick-beamed framework, covered with cabers, supported the weight of the heavy roof. A cluster of small cottages stood further up the brae. The simple stonewalls of these buildings was tightly packed with a mixture of peat and sand. If this infill could be kept damp – no great difficulty in this climate – the walls would act as a heat exchange unit, keeping the houses warm in winter and cool in summer.

The present Portkil farmhouse was built for the Duke of Argyll's chamberlain, a very important person who oversaw the estate management. In 1942, an American military hospital was built on the site. After the war this complex was taken over and used as accommodation by the Royal Navy, until demolition in the early 1950s. Now rows of beehives, producing Portkil honey, stand on the concrete bases.

Portkil Gun Battery was emplaced more than a century ago, guarding the busy shipping lanes of the Clyde estuary. The guns, however, have remained completely silent throughout their lives – except when the *Vital Spark* came under fire in one of the Parahandy episodes.

Portnellan

In this land of sea and lochs the name Portnellan is frequently found; *Port nan Eilean* simply means 'Port of the Island'. On the north shore of Loch Katrine is one Portnellan, into which Rob Roy MacGregor and his family crowded after their own house had been burned in the ferocious aftermath of the '15 rebellion.

It was to the island served by this Portnellan, the Black Isle, that

Rob Roy carried the Duke of Montrose's factor in 1716. James Graham was released 11 days later, quite unharmed and with all his documents intact – but relieved of the money he had been carrying. A MacGregor burial ground stretches out into Loch Katrine, the level having been raised several times, keeping the old bones safe from the increased capacity of Glasgow's reservoir.

Loch Dochart has another Portnellan, once the ferry point for the Campbell Castle on Eilean Iubhar (pronounced *ewar*) – the 'Island of Yews'. Long ago this was the stronghold of Taileachd, the mighty warrior who slew the great Finn McCoul. Finn's headless body drifted downriver to the Falls of Dochart, said to be his final resting place. One of several interpretations of Killin is *cill Fionn* – the burial ground of Finn.

Today this Portnellan is a complex of luxury lodges, cottages and bunkhouse accommodation. It offers the attraction of free use of boats, bicycles and canoes – and free fishing. There are other Portnellans in and around the Loch Lomond and Trossachs National Park, all with their own places in history and stories to be told.

Port of Menteith

A port can be a place where ships tie up, or may be a French word, one of many adopted through the Auld Alliance, meaning an entrance or gateway. Menteith is derived from the Gaelic word *moine* – a moss or moorland – linked to the Teith, a local river. Menteith was one of the five great regions into which early Scotland was divided. Menteith became an earldom in the 12th century, and the Port was elevated to burgh status by James III in 1466, becoming the Barony of Menteith.

The Port of Menteith lies at the north east corner of Scotland's only lake, under the long ridge of the Highland Boundary Fault. The Gothic style church was built in 1878, the west door incorporating part of a much older building. Unusually, Menteith church has a chime of bells. The ancient graveyard is the final resting place for several families with links to the old earldom. The Graham mausoleum is quite striking. A little to the south is the site of an early chapel, used when the water of the lake was too rough to permit worship at the priory on Inchmahome.

An act of the old Scottish Parliament stated that an inn should stand at each side of a ferry crossing, to offer shelter and sustenance to the traveller. The fine Lake Hotel is still keeping up its end of that bargain. A ferry continues to cross the lake to Inchmahome, but only during the summer months. King Edgar (1097–1106) is said to have commissioned a church for the island. The priory was built in 1238. Other visitors have included King Robert Bruce and Mary Queen of Scots.

The Port of Menteith is an excellent place for Osprey watching. These majestic birds nest nearby and take fish out of the lake.

Postbus

Postbus services have become a feature of many remote rural communities, often providing the only public transport to the outside world. Within the National Park, Callander has three postbus routes and Aberfoyle has two. The Callander postbuses connect with Killin, Ardeonaig, Crianlaraich and Tyndrum to the north, and through the Trossachs to Aberfoyle, to the west.

One Aberfoyle postbus runs the entire length of Strathard, along the infamous B829; 21 tortuous Scottish miles. Before the Act of Union in 1707, a Scottish mile was 1,948 yards. In this excursion the postbus will travel from the gentle lowlands into the very heart of the Scottish Highlands.

The route passes five Scottish glens, takes in six Scottish lochs, including the beautiful Loch Katrine and the vast Loch Lomond, and, on a clear day, lets you see five Scottish mountains of over 3,000 ft. At Inversnaid the road, now designated the C68, drops 400 ft in just a quarter of a mile, almost into Loch Lomond. Here walkers can disembark for the West Highland Way or the ferry to Inveruglas. This postbus also links to the midday sailing of the *Sir Walter Scott* from Stronachlachar.

The postbus provides a valuable service to the community and enables visitors to explore the wild upper reaches of Strathard without having to drive on the worst maintained roads in the country. It also gives passengers the chance to look around. Its route passes through the domains of the eagle and the wildcat – and much, much more besides.

Information may be obtained at Aberfoyle and Callander post offices or at www.royalmail.com/postbus

Pot of Gartness

Gart an eas is the Gaelic form of Gartness – an enclosure with a waterfall. The Gart is enclosed, almost encircled by the Endrick Water. The Pot of Gartness is a natural cauldron carved into the old red devonian sandstone, a rock stratum which stretches from the Highland Boundary Fault to the Kilpatrick Hills. The Endrick Water pours over a series of ledges and powers its way through a narrow cleft in the bedrock, an awesome spectacle when the river is in spate. Endrick comes from Gaelic *avon eiric* – river that rises.

Gartness came into the Napier family in 1495, and it was at Gartness castle that John Napier, the famous mathematician, is believed to have been born, in 1550. This is the man who blighted many a school day by inventing both logarithms and a slide rule known as Napier's Bones. Whenever the noise of the local mill disturbed Napier's concentration, he would simply have it shut down to give him perfect peace and tranquillity.

The West Highland Way passes through this secluded hamlet, crossing the modern bridge that replaced the one of 1715. Under the bridge are the vestiges of an old mill lade, evidence of the industrial past powered by this water. Several mill ruins can be seen, one of them incorporating old stone from the vanished medieval castle.

There are no bus services to the Pot of Gartness; the nearest routes pass through Drymen or Killearn, both within easy walking distance. It is well worth making an effort to visit the Pot of Gartness, especially in late August or early September when the salmon are leaping and fighting their way upstream to their spawning beds. Extra reward will be found at the excellent Wishing Well restaurant. Bon appetit!

Puck's Glen

Puck's Glen is concealed on the eastern hillside of Strath Eachaig, two miles south of Loch Eck. The name Puck's Glen was bestowed on this area by William 'Crimean' Simpson, who was the world's first official war artist. Simpson frequently painted in this magical glen. Shakespeare's Puck took his name from the Irish Puca and Welsh Pwcca, mischievous spirits who from earliest times enjoyed changing shape, misleading travellers, spoiling milk, frightening girls, and tripping up venerable old women.

A narrow footpath enters this wild cleft in the hillside, passing into a spooky woodland and following a tumbling burn. Tall pine, larch, cypress and redwood trees give cover to rhododendrons, ferns and moss-covered boulders. Halfway up, the forest offers an easy escape, while the top section becomes very challenging. Fallen trees add to the gloom – it is easy to see faeries hiding in every shadow.

There are several choices of paths that may be used to extend the experience, all eventually emerging to give glorious views of Highland peaks. There are links to both Kilmun Arboretum and Benmore Botanic Gardens. A long-distance walk crosses the hill to Gairletter Point on Loch Long.

The Bayley Balfour Memorial Hut, panelled with every variety of wood grown on the Benmore estate, has been removed from Puck's Glen and reassembled in the Benmore Gardens – but without its original chimney. This popular landmark is a fitting memorial to Balfour, the Professor of Botany who was Keeper of these Royal Botanic Gardens for 34 years.

Q

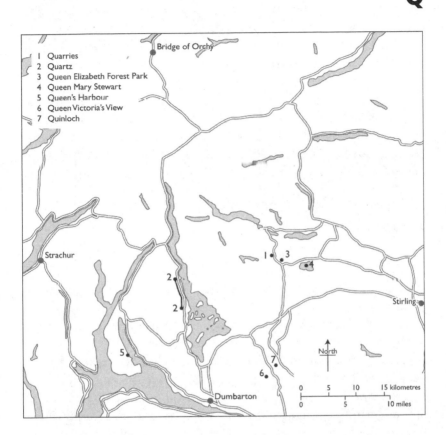

1 Quarries
2 Quartz
3 Queen Elizabeth Forest Park
4 Queen Mary Stewart
5 Queen's Harbour
6 Queen Victoria's View
7 Quinloch

Quadrantids

The Quadrantid meteor shower is one of the strongest of the year, regularly producing 50 to 120 meteors an hour in northern skies. The Quadrantids peak on or around 3 January and, although bright, are of relatively short duration. The meteorite shower emanates from the constellation Bootes, situated towards the north east quarter of the sky.

The name is derived from a now defunct constellation called Quadrans Muralis, somewhere between Draco, Hercules and Bootes.

In 1922 a number of constellations were removed from a crowded star atlas and the present list of 88 recognised constellations was adopted. The Quadrantids, nevertheless, retained their name.

The Quadrantid meteorites are unusual in having no known comet source. New evidence links them to asteroid 2003 EH1, a remnant of a comet that broke apart in deepest space, 500 years ago. The Earth passes quickly through the debris, which accounts for the brevity of the display. Particles captured by gravity – usually smaller than a grain of sand but occasionally several metres in diameter – become heated by friction. Molecules of gas are formed, becoming ionised and glowing as they destroy themselves in steaks of light.

Quadrantid shooting stars are travelling at 45 miles a second. Be in the right place at the right time, with a whisky in hand, looking into a star filled sky, and marvel!

Quarries

Man has quarried rock since the earliest Stone Age and the land is pockmarked with these excavations. Until it began to be shut down in the 1950s, Aberfoyle quarry was one of the largest in Europe. It is still very much a feature of the landscape today.

Aeons ago, tiniest particles of silt, including grains of hard quartz, settled in deep water. Eventually, buried to a great depth, pressure and heat metamorphosed this fine clay into slate. A bed of wonderfully wrought slate runs north east from Bute, through Aberfoyle, and on towards the North Sea. The quality of Aberfoyle slate was noted as far back as 1724, and was much sought after.

Slate cleaves or splits readily into thin slabs, exhibiting great strength and durability. Aberfoyle slate is found in three colours, each being the effect of different minerals. Iron oxide gives purple, iron sulphide makes dark blue, and chlorite produces green slate – the most popular choice.

In 1820, three workers produced 75 tons of slate. By 1858 output from Aberfoyle had reached 1.4 million slates. At that point there were more people living at the quarry settlement than in

Aberfoyle village. The railway was extended to Aberfoyle, to transport the local slate away to far-flung places. Then, far-flung slate came to Aberfoyle!

For many years Aberfoyle held its own against competition from Welsh slate. But eventually cheap imports of Spanish and (even cheaper) Chinese slate proved too much. Some stone is still taken, although nature has largely reclaimed the quarry complex. Many interesting walks can be found, including one from David Marshall Lodge. The Trossachs Trundler and postbus regularly pass the quarry.

Quartz

Veins of milky white quartz are clearly visible in the exposed rock cuttings on the A82, along Loch Lomondside. Quartz is the most indestructible and widespread of all rock forming minerals. The word quartz comes from a German mining term meaning hard, found in Middle High German as *quarc*. Quartz is made of silica (SiO_2) and coloured variations produce a wide range of gemstones, such as amethyst, cairngorm and rose quartz, much sought after for their beauty.

The hard hexagonal crystals can be turned into glass and ceramics, used as abrasives and made into cement. Quartz can also be crushed and dissolved in hydrogen cyanide to yield a harvest of silver and gold – a practice not unknown at Tyndrum. A recipe from 1675 says to boil the root of yellow iris in water and, when cool, hold a white pebble in the water and rub with a piece of iron. The water will become black and produce a tolerably good ink. Today, because of the piezoelectric effect, quartz is used as a regulator in radio transmitters and clocks and many other hi-tech products.

Veins of quartz formed in volcanic intrusions 350–400 million years ago, a period of great geological activity. Early man used quartz, in the form of flint, to make primitive tools and weapons, and it still finds use in lucky charms and healing stones. If you stoop to pick up a small stone that has caught your eye, the chances are that it will be a piece of pure white quartz.

Queen Elizabeth Forest Park

The Queen Elizabeth Forest Park commemorates the Coronation of Elizabeth II on 2 June 1953. At that time the forest covered 32,334 acres/13,085 hectares, stretching from Gleann Dubh, east across the Trossachs, to Loch Venachar. The following year, 9,500 acres/3,845 hectares at Rowardennan were added, taking the new Forest Park to the waters of Loch Lomond. Today the Queen Elizabeth Forest Park has grown to 50,000 acres/20,235 hectares and, like Topsy, is still growing.

In 1960, the chairman of the Carnegie Trust offered to hand over the ground above Aberfoyle, already supporting a well established woodland, to the Forestry Commission. The visitor centre carries his name, as the David Marshall Lodge. The exchange was by gentleman's agreement, done simply by letter – and not a lawyer in sight. David Marshall Lodge is a first class attraction, with a shop, a restaurant with wonderful views, a resident wood carver, and a live televised osprey watch. There is a small loch with ducks and swans, several picnic sites, a superb children's adventure play area and a whole range of walks. The longest and best of the way-marked routes is blue – the Highland Boundary Trail. If you have the stamina, it is well worth the effort.

In 1973 the Queen Mother unveiled a monument to mark the expansion of the Forestry Commission to one million acres in Scotland. The monument stands to the right of the approach to the lodge.

To celebrate the Queen's Silver Jubilee, an extensive forest drive was laid in the heart of the Queen Elizabeth Forest Park. The seven mile route wends its way through the trees, taking in three lochs and showing off some incredible scenery. Not to be missed!

Queen Mary Stewart

The variation Stuart derives from the French spelling *Steuart*, adopted at the time of Mary's marriage to the dauphin, in 1558. French had no W and only uses the letter in words borrowed from other languages.

During the English incursion, led by the earl of Hertford, to seize the young Queen of Scots, Mary was sheltered at Inchmahome Priory, on the Lake of Menteith. Henry VIII wanted four year old Mary as a bride for his eldest son, Prince Edward, and a very Rough Wooing ensued! All to no avail.

Accompanied by her mother, Mary of Guise, and the famous four Marys, the sojourn on the island retreat was relatively short. In a couple of weeks, helped by Mary Beaton, Mary Seton, Mary Fleming and Mary Livingston, the little queen is said to have built a chapel, designed a garden and planted an orchard.

What we find on Inchmahome today is Queen Mary's Chamber, situated above the Chapter House. Also evident is Queen Mary's Garden, a walled enclosure 30 yards square, to the south west of the historic ruins. Queen Mary's Bower, an oval den of box trees, can be seen on a mound between the Garden and the Lake. The Queen's Tree, a box tree in the centre of her Garden, which survived well into the 20th century, is no longer with us. Neither is the ancient thorn in the Bower – only a bench for people to sit. But a few of the edible chestnuts, perhaps planted by the queen's fair hand, stand gnarled and splendid in their grand old age.

Queen's Harbour

The waters of the Gare Loch are special in more ways than one, not least because they come directly under royal control. This is a Queen's Harbour, one of only two in Scotland (Rosyth is the other one). The Queen's Harbour Master operates from Faslane and is responsible for the safe navigation and berthing of all vessels in his area. QHM will liaise fully with all port authorities in the Clyde that come under his jurisdiction.

The Gare Loch is popular with sailing enthusiasts and windsurfers, and seems to be the venue of a summer-long regatta. With the ferries, cargo vessels, cruise liners, oil tankers and the old PS *Waverley* going 'doon the watter', the Clyde is a busy place. All this activity normally carries on quite unabated by time or tide.

With Faslane being a very busy naval base – the entire nuclear submarine fleet sails out of the Gare Loch – occasionally the QHM exercises his authority and runs up a signal, indicating closure of the restricted waters. This signal is a red light above two vertical green ones. By day, a red flag with a diagonal white stripe is also displayed. This action covers a designated, dog-leg channel through the Rhu Narrows, prohibiting all but naval movements.

The signals are well positioned and clear for all to see, day or night. Anybody who accidentally or deliberately transgresses these restrictions may be apprehended by a naval officer or the police. You have been warned.

Queen Victoria's View

The Queen's View, on the west side of the A809, is one of a great many Queen Victoria is said to have enjoyed. The great northward panorama sweeps along the Highland Boundary Fault, from the mountains of Argyll to the high tops of Breadalbane. Standing at the eastern extremity of the Kilpatrick Hills, with the Campsie Fells opposite, overlooking Strathblane, no view could ever have pleased her more.

This area was a favourite corner of her vast empire, especially following the death of her beloved Albert. While the young princes continued to enjoy their late father's pursuits of hunting, fishing and shooting at Balmoral, the queen and princesses would summer quietly in the Trossachs. Many of Queen Victoria's Progresses have been marked by white, cast-iron mile markers, with regally pointed tops. These can be seen throughout the area.

Looking left from her View, Queen Victoria would have observed the Queen's Seat, where, as a child, Queen Mary took her last proper look at Scotland for 18 years. She was on her way to France. The hill is now known as Thief's Hill – for many years it was a haven for robbers and bandits, until government troops routed them out. This action took place only a few years before Victoria's visit – Scotland was still not fully tamed.

The Balfron and Drymen to Glasgow buses pass the Queen's

View. There is a large car park, usually with a burned out wreck or two, an information board and, of course, a viewpoint. It is well worthwhile climbing over the style and walking the short distance to the ridge. The reward is a vista that takes your eye over Loch Lomond and into the heart of the Highlands. If it pleased the queen, it will certainly please you.

Quinloch

Quinloch comes from *caoin* or *caoine* – gentle. In the past it has been pronounced *Cuinyoch* and *Kinyoch*. The Quinloch is one of a series of farms on a springline to the west of the Blane valley, looking across to the Campsie Fells and the Glengoyne distllilery. The slopes are lined with trees, some of them quite ancient, hiding an old road now little more than a faint line on the map.

The West Highland Way passes through the Quinloch, following the line of the long defunct Blane Valley railway. Easy enough going here, but the Highlands are looming on the northern horizon. The land seems to be squeezed between two busy roads running south towards Glasgow, yet Quinloch remains an oasis of remarkable tranquillity.

Above, on the high ridge, is a small lochan that used to supply water for a mill and bakery in Milngavie. Here too are gun emplacements, put in at the end of World War II. The two houses at the roadside were known as the Gunsite Cottages. The guns were never fired in anger; some say they were never fired at all. The huge weapons have long gone and the deep, steep-sided gun pits are full of water – more of a danger to life now than they ever were! Someone has put a few trout in to eat the midge larvae, and perhaps grow to a decent size.

Edward VII often carried his gun across Quinloch, working over pointers bred and trained on the estate. These were prize-winning gun dogs. I am sure some of Glengoyne's finest malt would have been consumed at the end of the day – and maybe a dram or two of Glenmorangie, distilled in the Gentle Glen.

R

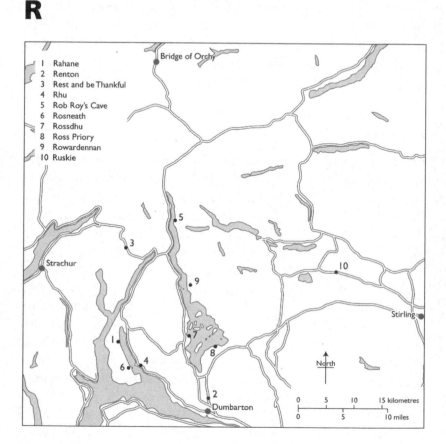

1 Rahane
2 Renton
3 Rest and be Thankful
4 Rhu
5 Rob Roy's Cave
6 Rosneath
7 Rossdhu
8 Ross Priory
9 Rowardennan
10 Ruskie

Rahane

Rahane comes from *rathain* – a ferny place. On the east side of the Isle of Rosneath, this linear development of houses and small farms looks across the Gare Loch to the Faslane Submarine Base. For centuries the waters of the Gare Loch sustained the local economies. Fishing provided most of the employment for Rahane; there was also a ferry across to Shandon. The fishing and the ferry have long gone and 21st century income is drawn from other sources.

In times gone past there were stories of great catches of fish being landed at Rahane. At times, it was said, the shoals were so big that a man might walk dry-shod across the loch. In 1510, the huge herring shoals brought in a school of basking sharks to feed on the fish. The sharks, in turn, attracted the attention of a 'Saurian Monster' that swam up and down the loch at great speed. With the head and neck of a giraffe, and the tail of a crocodile, the beast did everything except breath fire!

Also at Rahane, until quite recently, could be seen the markers for the measured mile. Ships built on the Clyde would undergo sea trials in the sheltered waters of the Gare Loch. In order to ascertain accurate speed-readings, the vessels would record their times between the Rahane Posts. Now it is all done by satellite. Because of a strange but quite local magnetic variation in this part of the Firth of Clyde, a line of buoys was laid in the Gare Loch, under the 1858 Navigation Act. Ships could anchor to one of the buoys, swing with the tide, and reset their compass before returning to sea.

Renton

Renton dates from 1762 and is named after Cecilia Renton, a lady who married a nephew of Tobias Smollett. The establishment of a large number of bleaching and printing works throughout the Vale of Leven led to the development of Renton, three miles upriver from the Clyde. The first library in the Vale opened at Renton in 1797. About 1820, the Cattle Fair moved to Renton from Dumbarton Muir. As many as 12,000 animals were traded, accompanied by ferocious running battles amongst the spectators.

Very little remains of the original Renton – just a few old houses on the east side of Main Street. Late Victorian development included the building of Renton Trinity parish church in 1891; a red sandstone construction with a pinnacled tower. Redevelopment during the 1920s, and again in the 50s and 60s, quite changed the face of Renton. The 60 ft Tuscan column, erected in 1774, has survived.

This is a memorial to the physician and novelist, Tobias Smollett, with an inscription by the great Dr Samuel Johnson.

Football seems to have been the lifeblood of the Vale. Renton was no exception, becoming one of the earliest members of the SFA, in 1873. Scottish Cup winners in 1888, Renton played and defeated West Bromwich Albion, their English counterparts – and became the first World Champions! Renton were soon to be beaten by their next door neighbours, the Vale of Leven, and blamed the referee. Now where have I heard that one before?

Rest and be Thankful

The 900 ft/274 m summit of the Rest and be Thankful is a place at which many a footsore traveller, and overheated vehicle, have taken their ease. The modern, well-graded A83 climbs steadily up Glen Croe from the shores of Loch Long, above the military road of 1748, built by the labours of the 24th regiment. Wordsworth described the rough stone seat erected here by the soldiers of General Johnnie Cope, as they constructed a road from Dumbarton to Inveraray.

The Rest and be Thankful is encircled by some of the finest peaks of Cowal. The northward ascent of Ben Ime, a Munro at 3,318 ft/1,011 m, usually starts from here. Clockwise, the eye takes in the Cobbler, the rocky slopes of the Brack, and, away to the west, the mass of Ben Donich – every one a Corbett. The westerly descent from the Rest and be Thankful passes lonely Loch Restil, under brooding Beinn an Lochain (2,985 ft/901 m).

The translation of Restil is often given as 'Point of the Lime Trees', from *ros teile*. There are trees – two alders, two rowans, a willow and a birch – but not a lime in sight. This is certainly not lime tree habitat. I prefer the derivation from *freastail*, the *f* being silent, meaning 'to wait upon'. From the earliest days, there would surely have been a hostelry of sorts to serve the needs of travellers and drovers.

At one time, the Duke of Argyll intended to route his road

from the head of Loch Long, up Glen Loin, past Ben Vane and down Glen Kinglas. This would have provided a longer but gentler gradient for horse drawn transport. Fortunately the plan never came to fruition, leaving motoring enthusiasts with one of the finest hill-climb roads in Scotland.

Rhu

On 7 March 1927, the anglicised spelling of Row reverted to Rhu, from the Gaelic *rudha* – a point of land. The parish of Rhu was established in 1648, with Aulay M'Aulay building a church and giving land for a manse and glebe. The present church dates from 1851 and was enlarged in 1891. With a school and a ferry, Rhu quickly grew in importance and the road to Dumbarton started from here. A coaching service ran from the Colquhoun Arms, now the Rhu Inn, and a bus company is still based in the village.

Many Highland families sailed to a new life from Rhu. One family, however, had a change of heart, settled in Rhu, and set up business. Dispossessed after Culloden, they took their name from their homeland, the Spey Valley. Now James and Colin Spy continue the family joinery firm from the original premises. Well, someone had to make and repair the essential oak casks.

When George IV demanded a taste of genuine Highland Dew, his Duke of Argyll came to Rhu Point. Here His Grace took delivery of whisky distilled in Aldownick Glen, a deep ravine behind the church. This location appears as Whistlers Glen in Walter Scott's *Heart of Midlothian* – after a curlew call given as a warning of Excise Men. As Highland whisky went out, West Indian rum came in. The local yachts were very busy, avoiding unjust tariffs and iniquitous taxes wherever they could.

Yachting is very much at the heart of Rhu. The simple stone pier of 1835 became a modern marina in 1977. The Royal Northern & Clyde Yacht Club is based at Ardenvohr, overlooking Rhu Narrows. A Coastguard Station opened in 1965 and a lifeboat is based at

Rhu. Some of the world's finest yachtsmen and women hoisted their first spinnaker on these waters.

Rob Roy's Cave

MacGregor lands extended down the eastern flank of Loch Lomond as far as Rowardennan, a rocky estate known as Craigroyston. In 1712, through rather foul means, Rob Roy MacGregor lost all his possessions to Graham of Montrose.

With his house burned and his family evicted, the fun really started. If Rob Roy could no longer trade as a legitimate cattle dealer, then he would live at the Duke of Montrose's expense. Soon fat cattle began to disappear from His Grace's farms, and grain out of his girnals. Montrose never knew where Rob Roy would strike next, and the bandit quickly went to ground after each raid in one of his numerous caves.

One cave is less than a mile north of Inversnaid Hotel, along the West Highland Way. A flight of steps cut into the path, adjacent to a perpendicular rock face, is directly above the well-hidden entrance. A small track leads over a jumble of boulders, very slippery in wet weather. From the water, the word CAVE can be seen, in large white letters, identifying the exact location of this famous refuge. It's not very big, but it is dry.

Rob Roy's Cave is the haunt of the feral goats of Inversnaid, direct descendants of the animals that saved the life of Robert Bruce in 1306. Hunting for Bruce, a pack of hounds entered the cave and flushed out a small group of goats. The pursuers wrongly assumed the cave to be empty and left without any further investigation. The present goats should be left to enjoy the peaceful grazing, granted to them by Royal Charter in 1314.

Rosneath

Rosneath is the chief settlement on the YL of Rosneath. In the 6th century, St Modan founded a church on the west side of the Gare

Loch. In 1230, the monks of Paisley Abbey built a church at Rosneath in return for the fishing rights of the whole of the Gare Loch – but only with nets. This was a lease granted by the Earl of Lennox.

In 1489 the Campbells swept down the yl of Rosneath and seized control. They planted a Campbell castle at Rosneath, from where they could exercise full power over the Gare Loch and Clyde. The Campbell castle was destroyed by fire in 1802, and the 5th Duke of Argyll built a new and very ornate replacement, itself demolished in 1961. The site is now a caravan park – such is progress!

The present church dates from 1853 and has the bell from an earlier building on display. This bell, cast by Ian Burgerhuis in 1610, was rung as the Call to Arms at the 1715 uprising. Buried at Rosneath is a freed slave from the Caribbean. Also, in the old churchyard, is the grave of Moses McNeil, a founding father of Glasgow Rangers. Every stone at St Modan's has a story to tell.

The sea has always played a large part in the life of Rosneath, especially before the advent of roads. Clyde ferries and pleasure steamers plied their trade, and the wartime activity of shipping and seaplanes made Rosneath a busy place indeed. Vessels were degauzed here, static electricity removed, to prevent them triggering mines. In yacht building terms, Rosneath is up there with the best of them. Some of the finest yachts ever built were launched from Silver's yard. Now Lifeboats come for servicing and repair.

Rossdhu

Rossdhu, on the west side of Loch Lomond, is the Dark Promontary, so called from the time the land was covered with heath. The heather was removed in 1780 and good soil brought in to improve the pasture to a lighter grassland. The present house, home to the Colquhouns, was built in 1773 and is haunted by two ghosts. Close by are the ruins of an older castle and a 12th century chapel. An even earlier stronghold stood offshore, on the manmade crannog of Ellan Rossdhu.

Alexander II granted the Barony of Colquhoun, in Dunbarton-shire, to Kilpatrick. Ingram of this line married the heiress of Luss and settled at Rossdhu. Mary Queen of Scots hunted here with Sir John Colquhoun, who was deeply implicated in her plotting against Elizabeth of England. During World War I, Sir Iain Colquhoun kept a fairly tame lion with him in the trenches. He was sentenced to death for allowing his men to fraternise with the enemy – they played football on Christmas Day. Fortunately, Sir Iain was pardoned by George V.

The Loch Lomond Golf Club has taken a hundred year lease from Colquhoun Estates, and the course, designed by Tom Weiskopf, opened in 1994. Apart from a few extra water features, the course is one of the finest in Scotland. There is a public footpath the entire length of the estate, but the golf course and the Rossdhu clubhouse are only visible from the northern end, and from the waters of Loch Lomond.

Not far from the 18th green is an excellent example of an ice-house – an early form of refrigeration.

Ross Priory

Ros can mean promontory, headland or cape, but also wood or, as an elided form of *riasg*, moor, fen or bog. An abbey was founded on the south shore of Loch Lomond about 700 AD. Later elevated, Ross functioned as a priory until the Reformation. In 1625 Ross Priory became the seat of one of the septs of Buchanan. The oldest part of the house is 14th century, but most of the building dates from the late 1700s.

The Buchanan tenure came to an end through the power of a curse. In the aftermath of Culloden, Murray of Tulliebardine sought refuge at Ross Priory. On being betrayed, Tulliebardine foretold that one day there would still be Murrays on Atholl and not a Buchanan at Ross. One by one the family lines failed, and now Strathclyde University has possession of the Priory.

Walter Scott was a frequent guest at Ross Priory, working on his epic poem, 'Lady of the Lake', and his best selling novel, *Rob Roy*. Sir Walter would have walked the short distance to the vanished village of Aber, marked only by a stone paved road and a few cultivated roses. He must have strolled many times through the well-tended priory gardens; these are open to the public for one Sunday in May. Visitors now come to Ross Priory to play golf, sail or just enjoy the views into the Highlands.

In June 1971, the Queen pressed a button at Ross, inaugurating a new water scheme. Every day, 50 million gallons (250 million litres) of Loch Lomond water are pumped out to slake the thirst of Central Scotland. This can be doubled, if required.

Ross Priory is within easy walking distance of the bus stop at Gartocharn.

Rowardennan

At Rowardennan, on the east shore of Loch Lomond, the B837 comes to an end. Only forest tracks and the West Highland Way venture further north, along the wooded lochside. Rowardennan comes from *Rutha aird Eunain*, 'the High Point of St Eunan' (a shortened form of Adamnan, biographer of St Columba). The 'Polo Mint' monument marks the fact that Rowardennan is part of a memorial to the dead of all wars.

The summer ferry from Inverbeg is the only direct means of public transport. The alternative is an eight mile walk from either Inversnaid or Balmaha. Rowchnock, in times past, was 'the Point of the Shout' – from which the ferry would be hailed. Many cattle, destined for lowland trysts, would be swum across the narrow stretch of water at this point.

Close to the pier stands the much-improved Rowardennan Hotel, with its highly recommended cuisine. This is the most popular starting point for the four mile hike to the top of Ben Lomond (3,194 ft/974 m), the most southerly of all Munros.

The narrow road passes Ross Wood and Ross Point and the Glasgow University field station. Here studies are made into every life form found in the loch, from microscopic zooplankton to the 13 species of fish. The Ross Isles, a chain of small islands, shelter some of the finest sea trout and salmon fishing. From Rowardennan, the West Highland Way skirts Rob Roy's Prison and then Rowchoish, from which point children used to make their way to Inversnaid school. Records show their attendance was rather sporadic.

This is real Rob Roy country, as wild now as it was then. A quarter of all British flowering and non flowering plants are to be found here. Look out for the local feral goats, which enjoy eating most of them.

Ruskie

Between Port of Menteith and Thornhill lies Ruskie, a cluster of traditional farms along the sunny south face of the Menteith Hills. Ruskie is derived from the Gaelic *riascach* – a boggy place. Below is Flanders Moss, once a sodden morass as it emerged from the retreating North Sea. Traces of a Roman road and outlines of ancient fortification are testimony to the importance of this dry ridge in times long past.

Directly north is Loch Rusky (an alternative spelling found as far back as 1472). This small loch, below the escarpment of Ben Gullipen, belongs to Heriot Watt University. The waters provide some of the best trout fishing in Scotland and the wet margins produce a wonderful array of wild flowers. On a crannog in Loch Rusky once stood the tower of Sir John Stewart, the False Menteith who betrayed William Wallace to the English.

The A873 from Ruskie merges with the A81, which has passed Loch Rusky, at Rednock. The road continues towards the Lake of Menteith, enshrined in an English name to perpetuate the memory of John Stewart's treachery. Fragmentary remains of Rednock Castle can be seen adjacent to a neat farm steading. Built in the 16th century by the Grahams of Menteith, only the round stair turret is still standing. Pony trekking has been added to the more usual farming enterprises of sheep and cattle.

The Stirling-Aberfoyle bus serves both Ruskie and Rednock, and, during the summer season, the Trossachs Trundler passes Loch Rusky.

S

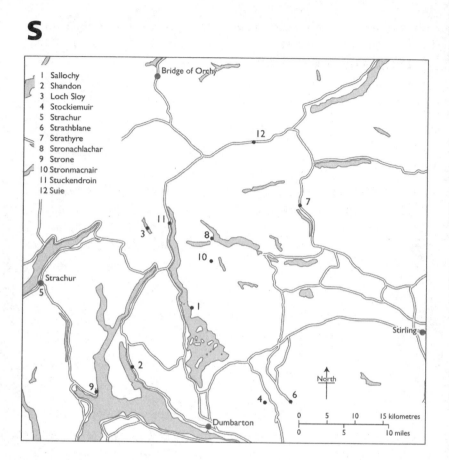

1 Sallochy
2 Shandon
3 Loch Sloy
4 Stockiemuir
5 Strachur
6 Strathblane
7 Strathyre
8 Stronachlachar
9 Strone
10 Stronmacnair
11 Stuckendroin
12 Suie

Sallochy

Sallochy is on the east side of Loch Lomond, just where the waters narrow and the loch takes on a fjordic appearance. The name comes from *salach* – dirty – though this probably refers to the place being dank and gloomy, rather than unclean. Between the lie of the land and thick tree cover, direct sunlight seldom reaches ground level. Sallochy Wood is at the western extremity of the Queen Elizabeth Forest, and is part of the Ben Lomond War Memorial Park.

Sallochy is a very special place – almost a nature reserve in its own right. Squeezed between the loch and the foothills of Ben Lomond, and with abundant water always beneath the oak trees and conifer plantation, wildlife thrives. The beautiful, sleek, red-coated pine marten has returned to the upper canopy and has begun to make inroads against the population of alien grey squirrels. But concrete nest-boxes are now required to keep out the pine martens. Bird life ranges from the tiny goldcrest wren to the turkey sized capercailzie – Gaelic for 'horse of the forest'. The water supports a host of plants and at least 10 species of dragon and damselflies This is a naturalist's paradise.

A small road runs through Sallochy, towards Rowardennan. The West Highland Way passes this way, too. Of late, Sallochy has become a very popular, if unofficial, camping site – with all the attendant problems. In the long term, proper facilities are required. In the short term, the Forestry Commission intends closing it down. There are several excellent walks in and around Sallochy; to the old slate quarry, to Dun Mor and Dun Maoile, and to the quiet waters of the Dubh Lochan.

Shandon

Shandon is one of the innumerable developments that snake almost seamlessly around the north shore of the Clyde, within easy sailing distance of Glasgow. The Age of Steam made commuting possible, first by ferry and later by train. The Industrial Revolution brought untold wealth to Glasgow – and severe pollution. Those who could afford to, simply moved out of town. The local population of farming and fisher folk were soon joined by colonies of very rich neighbours.

Shandon is 'the Old Fort', from *sean* – old – and *dun* – a fort. The remains of the dun can be found exactly one mile due north of Stuckenduff Farm. Also on the west side of this steep ridge, over-looking the Gare Loch, are stones with ancient cup and ring markings.

The Earls of Lennox had one of their many castles at Shandon, now obliterated by progress. Modern redevelopment has even robbed Shandon of many of the earlier mansions, built in the Marine Genre.

The A814 was widened and re-routed in 1969, to meet the requirements of Her Majesty's Naval Bases at Coulport and Faslane. The pier, built in 1860, had to be demolished. It was unique amongst the piers of the Clyde, having been constructed from criss-cross iron girders on massive timber supports. The old Free Church marks the site of the pier. Built in 1844, with a tower added in 1883, it was closed in 1981 and converted into four apartments. The kirk was itself converted from the malthouse of Altdonaig distillery. This, alas, has also been lost to us.

The rock strewn beach is fine for walking when the tide is out, as is the long section of the old main road. This doubles up as a cycle track and is a popular dog exercise area, well shaded along its entire length by massive trees.

Loch Sloy

Loch Sloy was a wild and remote place before it was subdued by the hand of man. Loch Sloy was both the war cry and the gathering ground of the turbulent MacFarlanes, who mustered on an island on the shallow loch, now lost under 150 ft/47 m of dammed water. Sloy takes its name from the Slaugh, a host of spirits who, with a *gan* – a great shout – could rouse sleeping mortals and carry them off into the night. The victims of the Slaugh would be made to do things they would not normally dream of. An advertising *slogan* is meant to do exactly the same thing!

In 1943, the North of Scotland Hydro Electric Board began to harness the natural power of water. Loch Sloy holds the British All Comers Rainfall record; between 17 and 18 January 1974, 9.9 inches (238 mm) of rain fell in just 24 hours. The dam between Ben Vane and Ben Vorlich was largely built by Prisoners of War. Opened by the Queen on 18 October 1950, Loch Sloy water surges through a two mile (3.2 km) tunnel into the four massive pipes lying exposed on the side of Ben Vorlich. 160 kilowatts of electricity can be generated each day for the National Grid.

One route to the reservoir starts at Succoth, where Glen Loin runs into Loch Long. Succoth, in Gaelic, means a place on a point of land between two rivers. In biblical terms, it was the way by which the Israelites went out of Egypt. A good path leads around the lower slopes of Beinn a' Chrois, joining the service road to the dam, from Inveruglas. Hardier walkers can set out from the car park alongside the A83, at Butterbridge, and climb through Glen Kinglas, eventually reaching Loch Sloy.

Stockiemuir

Coming from the south, the impact of the Stockiemuir is equivalent to the very first sip of a fine malt whisky. It quite takes your breath away. After the initial impression, just like a 10 year old Glengoyne, you have to search for the hidden depths. In the distance is the Highland massif and a tantalising glimpse of Loch Lomond. Above is one of the biggest skies you will ever see and, before you, a vast expanse of moorland. This is a wild area of peat, heather, encroaching bracken and outcropping rock.

Stockiemuir could well be derived from the Gaelic *stuic* – stump(y) – and *monadh* – a mountain, of which there are several candidates. The Stockiemuir is itself almost totally surrounded by other moors; six in all. Every one has a *stuic* or two. There is not much sign of life, only the odd blackface sheep and, occasionally, men flying model aeroplanes. But the hand of earlier peoples can easily be found. A vitrified fort tops an outcrop on Quinloch Muir, to the east, and Stockiemuir has standing stones and chambered cairns – a history stretching back over 5,000 years.

The A809, running north from Glasgow, traces the line of the 1796 Turnpike Road. This would have followed the route taken by the cattle droves, selecting the driest possible way across the moor.

Other drove roads can be seen on the Stockiemuir, from Dumbarton Muir to the west, and from the north over Cameron Muir. There are even older roads, hollow tracks from the times of the first settled farming. Whether following one of these old roads or rambling across the moor, the Stockiemuir is superb.

This is the haunt of grouse and hen harrier, home to hidden waterfalls and, to the west, the Gates of Sodam and Lot's Wife, guarding Auchenreoch Glen. Spend enough time on Stockiemuir and you will soon realise that it has all the depth and character of a cask-strength Glengoyne whisky.

Strachur

The A815 traces an ancient route into the heart of Argyll, north from the Clyde, past Loch Eck and threading its way through a knot of hills to the Clachan of Strachur, overlooking Loch Fyne. More recent development has stretched Strachur someway along the water-front, with impressive views across the loch. The defunct pier, below Creagan an Eich, no longer serves the ferry from Inveraray. The well known Creggans Inn still provides hospitality to passing travellers. A former landlord, Sir Fitzroy MacLean, is believed to have been the real James Bond – he and Ian Fleming were at school together.

At one time known as Kilmaglass, 'Church of the Dear Grey Monk', the present name of Stachur comes from *strath* – a valley – and *corr* – a heronry. There are certainly plenty of herons, some stalking their prey in the shallows of Loch Fyne, others hunting in one of the two rivers. Eas Dubh runs north into the sea, while the River Cur takes the opposite direction to Loch Eck. Strachur held two large cattle fairs, on the last Saturday in May and the first Tuesday in October. The hardy animals were eventually destined for distant lowland markets.

The site of a Pictish dun overlooks the clachan from the north. The church, with a birdcage belfry, dates from 1789. The burial ground is very much older. Some of the ancient grave slabs have been set into the church wall, near to the door. The smithy has been restored to full working order and opens in the tourist season. Look out for a pair of relocated rowan trees, gracefully entwined. They were moved to their new site during the road improvements. Rowans are planted to ward off evil spirits and it is known to be exceedingly dangerous to do them any harm.

Strathblane

Strathblane is 12 miles north of Glasgow. First mention was made in the early 13th century but, judging from the ancient standing stones, Strathblane could be a great deal older. As part of the earldom of Lennox, Strathblane was one of seven Dunbartonshire parishes that became annexed to Stirling County. Fighting men and women from this area continue to enlist at Dumbarton. The village is now a fusion of three older hamlets; Mugdock, Netherton and Edenkill.

Strathblane is, as the name suggests, a fertile farming area. It means 'the Wide Valley of Little Flowers', from *strath* and *bladhach* – flowery. These rich farms were frequently plundered by northern clans. The MacGregor Watch would then be called in to recover any missing stock, which they did with great efficiency, on one occasion returning a flock of 200 sheep, only one animal short! An annual livestock fair was held at Edenkill every November until the 1880s.

The Industrial Revolution arrived with the bleaching and printing works, and the railway. Although this Age had long passed, nobody told the Germans. On a March night in 1941, Strathblane was bombed. A house at Sunnyside was hit, resulting in four fatalities. Strathblane did have a top-secret establishment, a covert railway station. This had been built at Dumgoyach, opposite Duntreath, so that Edward VII could visit his mistress! The lady was the sister of Sir Archibald Edmonstone of Duntreath, and great grandmother of Mrs Parker Bowles, the Duchess of Cornwall.

Another feature is the Gowk Stone. A gowk is a cuckoo, it is also a fool, and foolish things have taken place at the Gowk Stone. Anyone who slides three times down the Gowk Stone becomes a citizen of Strathblane.

Strathyre

Strathyre derives from *strath* – a wide valley – and *thire* – corn land. An old Gaelic prayer from Strathyre ends with the exhortation, 'Let my land turn white (with corn), lest we starve!' Oats would have been the main crop, well able to ripen in this deep, sun-shaded valley. Farming is still a feature of Strathyre, along with tourism and forestry. The vast Strathyre Forest was developed during the Depression years of the 1930s. In 1968, 8,000 trees were lost in the Great Blast, but eight million survived! The trees seem to climb to the very tops of the surrounding hills.

The dark conifers stand brooding over the busy A84, carrying commerce and visitors deep into the Highlands. The River Balvaig flows south through the village, passing under the old bridge that leads to the quiet side of the strath. Here the closed railway line has become a footpath and a section of National Cycle Route 7. The narrow road continues towards Stroneslaney and Balquhidder. Stroneslaney is the site of a bloody battle, fought in the thirteenth century, between the Buchanans and the local McLarens.

A memorial to the Gaelic poet and evangelist, Dugald Buchanan, stands in the Main Street of his birthplace. Also first seeing the light of day in Strathyre, was Bruce of Kinnaird. Bruce, red haired and a massive 6 ft 4 in tall, became an African explorer. He thought that he had discovered the elusive source of the Nile – he had not, of course, and died in 1794, a saddened man.

Overlooked by Beinn an-t-sidhean, 'the Faery Hill', Bonnie Strathyre has several fine hostelries and a village shop to fulfil the needs of its many visitors.

Stronachlachar

The scattered community of Stronachlachar is situated at the western end of Loch Katrine, eight miles by water from the Trossachs Pier. Six days a week, during the summer sailing season, the *Sir Walter Scott* comes sedately in to Stronachlachar pier, at 11.45am. At noon she begins her return journey, sailing against the most magnificent backdrop anywhere in Scotland. Some of the disembarked passengers face a 13 mile walk or cycle ride back to the east end of the loch. The postbus from Aberfoyle links with the steamer at Stronachlachar.

In Gaelic, *sron* is a nose or a point, *chlachair* is a mason. So, *Sron a'Chlachair* means 'the Stonemason's Point'. This is a very old name, perhaps from the time when ancient sacred stones were hewn and engraved with cup and ring marks. The name certainly pre-dates the stone built houses of Glasgow's Water Authority, constructed after 1856. An older farming township, with adjacent lazybeds, can be seen further up the hillside. This was MacGregor country; Rob Roy was born and raised at Glengyle, three miles further up the loch.

Stronachlachar used to be a marvel to behold, whether you were arriving by road or by steamer. The rhododendrons were box-trimmed, the grass was neatly mown, and everything that could be painted was bright and pristine. Now, with the workforce savagely reduced, the place has an air of neglect and despondency. Water Board houses, which stood empty for long enough, are at last being sold – but well beyond the means of anyone local. The school is down to a handful of children, the church is closed for worship and, along with the people, all the sheep have gone from the hills. This has been a 21st century Clearance.

Strone

Strone comes from Gaelic *sron*, meaning a nose, a point or a headland. There are many Strones and they come in divers guises, but only one is a village – the Strone projecting sharply between the Holy Loch and Loch Long. If you steer a southerly course from Strone Point, the next landfall will be Spain. Strone is typical of the Victorian ribbon development that flourished along the northern shores of the Firth of Clyde. The pier, opened in 1847, provided for the ferry to the outside world.

A chain of maritime villas and ornate cottages faces the sea. Along Shore Road, a striking lodge reflects the grandeur of the extravagant Baronial mansion dominating the skyline above. This was the Sailing Lodge of the Coates family, of Paisley Cotton fame. There is an easy to miss road, climbing steeply to a hillside terrace and more villas. Here, too, is a nine hole golf course, carved out of the rock and teed off in 1896. Never mind the golf; the views over the estuary are magnificent.

History has been recorded in the names on the landscape. Stronchullin may well refer to a great Irish warrior called Chulain, who was served by the hero, Cuchulain, a name meaning 'the Hound of Chulain'. Nearby is Cnoc nam Fiontann, 'the Hill of the Finn'. This has been identified as the site of an ancient Caledonian fort. From the top of either Blairmore or Blairbeg Hill, the strategic importance of Strone can be fully appreciated, protected as it is by the mountains, and defended by the sea.

Stronmacnair

Yet another of the many abandoned communities, this one perched on the nose of a hill. The ruins of Stronmacnair stand roofless and forlorn at the southern spur of Beinn Dubh, in the heart of Gleann Dubh. This is not 'the Dark Glen' but 'the Secret Glen', *dubh* being used in the sense of 'a dark secret'. Surrounded by a circle of mountains, Gleann Dubh has given shelter to countless generations of natives who have been born and died here, and to many others who have come for sanctuary.

Mary Queen of Scots was hidden here as a young child. Wallace and Bruce both sheltered their forces in the glen, at different times, and the surviving Templars fled here from Europe to regroup.

The last inhabitants, a mother and daughter, left Stronmacnair in 1961, moving to a brand new council house in Drymen. Not liking her modern bathroom, the mother would return to her old home, to bathe in the traditional manner – in a tin bath in front of a roaring peat fire. When the last fire went out, the house soon died and Stronmacnair became just a name on a map. *MacNair* means 'Son of the Fair One' and is a sept of the ancient MacFarlane clan.

Stronmacnair lies tucked in on the east side of Ben Lomond. Many of the departed found their final repose in the small burial ground. A modern, walled graveyard, just 350 years old, stands in a medieval cemetery, overlying a Neolithic burial cairn. There is also a Mesolithic stone altar – used long ago for human sacrifice. People have been buried on this small site since time immemorial. It's no wonder that Stronmacnair is reputed to be the most haunted place in Scotland.

Stuckendroin

A long time ago there lived two great rival bulls, one on each side of Loch Lomond, which would roar challenges back and forth across the water. The white bull on the east belonged to Clan Gregor, the red bull on the west to the MacFarlanes. One dark night, the white bull came around the head of the loch and, by first light, was ready to engage his adversary in mortal combat. The two powerful animals collided at full speed, locking horns on the hillside above Stuckendroin. Fur flew and the earth trembled!

The battle was so violent that an entire mountain disappeared, trampled down to form the Little Hills now standing in its place. A mass of rock, earth and boulders crashed down to the lochside, almost completely separating the north end from the rest of Loch Lomond. Even today, a single track of road, controlled by traffic lights, picks its way through the debris. Finally, the body of the red bull tumbled down the mountain and landed, broken, in a bog. The white bull contemptuously tossed down an enormous boulder to cover the final resting place of his vanquished foe, and retuned home.

That very large rock became known as Clach nan Tarbh, 'Stone of the Bull', and lies half a mile south of Stuckendroin Farm, between the A82 and the West Highland railway. Later it became the Pulpit Rock, first used for secret services by the persecuted Covenanters. In 1825 worship at the rock was resumed. A vestibule was blasted out, to provide shelter for the minister and precentor, who led the singing. There was no church building until 1895.

The scars on the landscape have long since healed and grown over. Stuckendroin, from *stuc* – a conical or steep rock – and *droigheann* – a thorny hill – is a peaceful Highland farm with sheep and cattle – and much quieter bulls.

Suie

Suie is the phonetic rendition of *suidh* – a seat, as in a place of learning. This name is a direct link to the eighth century and the cult of St Fillan. From earliest times, food and shelter could be obtained at this holy site, the monks seeing to the needs of any traveller. In the later, secular period, hospitality was still provided to those who came this way. There is mention of an inn at Suie in the 16th century. Two hundred years later the Campbells of Breadalbane built a hunting lodge alongside the new military road through Glen Dochart. Given a Gothic remodelling in the 19th century, it has become the Suie Lodge Hotel.

St Fillan and his followers had an enormous and lasting influence on the history of this country. The seven sacred relics of Fillan were entrusted to men who became known as Dewars, each with their own free held land. The Dewar na Bernan, 'Keeper of the Bell', held his land at Suie. The Dewar's lands were lost but the bell has survived, now displayed in the National Museum, Edinburgh. Oaths were often made over the Bronze Age bell, and the penalty for default was madness. However, lunatics could also be cured, by wearing the bell as a helmet and lying all night on a stone! The large number of Celtic stones throughout Glendochart and Strathfillan indicates the importance of this route to and from deepest Argyll.

Suie offers many activities, especially fishing and walking. Coirechaorach, one of Rob Roy MacGregor's numerous houses, is close at hand. Slightly further is Ben More, the highest mountain south of Ben Nevis.

T

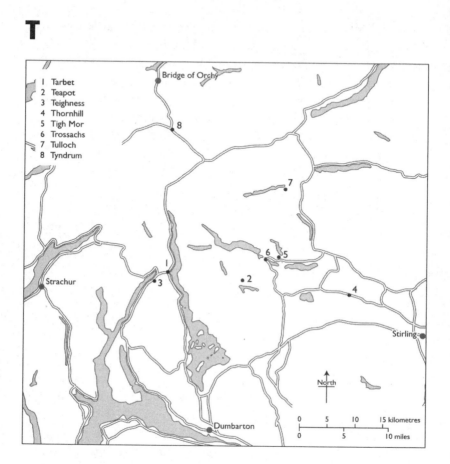

1 Tarbet
2 Teapot
3 Teighness
4 Thornhill
5 Tigh Mor
6 Trossachs
7 Tulloch
8 Tyndrum

Tarbet

Tarbet, on Loch Lomond, is at the eastern end of a narrow strip of land – on the western side is Arrochar, on Loch Long. *Tairbeart* signifies an isthmus and is a compound Gaelic noun meaning 'carrying across'. September 1263 saw 50 Viking longboats carried from Loch Long and launched on Loch Lomond. Taking battle formation in the lee of Tarbet Isle, the fleet sailed to pillage and lay waste to the entire area – an activity at which the Vikings truly excelled.

In 1326 Tarbet was raided again, this time by Robert Bruce. The king required 100 great trees for use on his own estates. More recent visitors have been of a kinder disposition, arriving by car, bus and train to enjoy the peace and tranquillity, and the outstanding scenery. The weather, it seems, never changes. On a wet October day in 1771, Thomas Russell composed a poem about his ascent of Ben Lomond – all 36 lines etched onto the hotel parlour window. It survived more than 50 years, but eventually a less perishable site was required.

Tarbet benefits from the shelter of the mountains, including Ben Lomond directly to the east. Loch Lomond – the third deepest freshwater body in Britain, here sounding 105 fathoms (630 ft/192 m) – and the Gulf Stream coming ashore 1.5 miles to the west, help to maintain an equable climate. Visitors can participate in a range of holiday activities, or simply relax. Tarbet is renowned for its pike fishing, using fresh caught mackerel, from Arrochar, as bait. Cruises on the loch leave from Tarbet pier. Today, the only boats out on the water are there purely for pleasure.

Teapot

The word 'teapot' is self-explanatory. As a place name on a map, however, it is a bit of a conundrum. The Teapot is halfway between Aberfoyle and Stronachlachar, on the B829, which runs the length of beautiful Strathard. It was here that coaches full of tourists would stop to rest and water the horses – and the passengers. If a pot of tea were ordered, a pot of tea would be served. However, if a *teapot* were ordered, out would come a pot full of whisky. Locally distilled, of course.

A township developed at this sheltered spot, more than six centuries ago, not long after the arrival of the Irish Gaels. These people farmed the land and built themselves turf-roofed houses. One unusual aspect of this area is that all the houses are on one side of the River Forth. Across the water, opposite the Teapot, stood the abode of the Wise Women of Strathard – the MacAlpines. These local witches had never been known to be mischievous or malevolent in any way, but I am sure the people of Kinlochard slept more soundly in their beds, knowing they were protected by running water.

The oak trees on the hill behind the Teapot were originally planted by James v. Like his father before him, James iv, he was an inveterate castle builder. Many stands of oak were established to ensure future supplies of timber for the royal castles and palaces of Scotland. Trees were recently taken from the Teapot and used in the restoration of the Great Hall at Stirling Castle.

By taking the track opposite the Teapot, over the bridge and past the solitary whitewashed house, it is possible to access many fine walks through Lochard forest. It will be quite safe – the Wise Women are long gone.

Teighness

Teighness is an age-old settlement at the headwater of Loch Long, now almost swallowed up by neighbouring Arrochar. The name is displayed on the general store and carried on the specially bottled malt whisky. The settlement is marked on the map as Tighness, simply a variation of the spelling. *Tigh na Eas* means 'House of the Waterfall' and there is a crystal clear burn through the town, plunging down the hillside and into the sea. Above the railway line, the water has been dammed to form a small reservoir.

Tigh is a word that even non-Gaelic speaking Scots will know the meaning of, but this little word has unexpected depths. In Greek it appears as *tekt* – to make or to build, as in 'architect'. Latin has it as *tectus* – to be covered – and *tectum* – a roof – from which the English take thatch and, via French, tile. Even the Finns have *tehda* – to do or to make. So *tigh* – to make or build something with a roof – a house.

It would have been at Teighness that, in September 1263, the Vikings lifted their boats, carrying them over to harry Loch Lomond.

In 1659, a new parish was formed, saving a great deal of walking to and from Luss. In 1733, at the time of the 5th minister, a church was built at Teighness, endowed on God's Acre by the MacFarlanes. The present church dates from 1847. It was here, in 1910, that the Admiralty established a torpedo range and experimental station, at one time employing 70 men but now lying idle over the loch.

There are old photographs of Teighness hanging on the walls in the Village Inn, winner of the Real Ale Pub of the Year for Dumbarton and Argyll. Sit with a glass in your hand and take in the views of Loch Long and the magnificent Arrochar Alps

Thornhill

Thornhill was founded on 10 February 1696, when Archibald Napier granted 15 feus of land on the thorn-covered ridge, immediately west of Norrieston. The development has uniquely maintained the original planned layout of straight main street with feus extending north and south. Each feu was 21 ells (20 m) by 66 ells (62 m), enough ground to enable the householder to grow vegetables and keep a cow. There was also Common Land, still enjoyed by the villagers, north and south of Thornhill.

Many black cattle came out of the north, through Aberfoyle, and along the dry ridge towards Stirling. Napier set out to exploit this passing trade by establishing a weekly market and four annual selling fairs, each to last eight days. A droving inn opened at Springfield, to augment services provided by the 1635 coaching house, now the Lion & Unicorn. The military road to the garrison at Inversnaid was pushed through in 1713. The Moss was laboriously cleared and rich arable land exposed. Thornhill prospered.

Apart from agriculture, there was weaving and tanning providing employment within Thornhill. Others were engaged at the nearby Deanston cotton works. The village had a corn mill, only closed in 1956, and two smithies. Queen Victoria had one of her horses re-shod here, after which time the smithy became known as Balmoral – and the smith's house called The Palace. The Devil was here too. He came to do a deal with Robert Napier of Ballinton, a famous alchemist searching for the secret of everlasting life. On failing to reach agreement, the Master of Darkness leapt from an upper window and vanished into the night!

Tigh Mor

Tigh Mor is set at the core of the Trossachs, overlooking Loch Achray and the dense cover of the Queen Elizabeth Forest Park. Formerly known as the Trossachs Hotel, Tigh Mor started life as Ardcheanocrochan, meaning 'a Farm with High Land at the Top of a Knoll' – Ben A'an. Tigh Mor means 'Big House'. Not only is Tigh Mor of considerable size, the impressive stone building has been adorned with candle-snuffer turrets. The design was by G.P. Kennedy, who also drew up plans for the nearby church and worked on the re-building of the Houses of Parliament.

After Sir Walter Scott had opened up the Trossachs to the tourist trade, Ardcheanocrochan quickly became a busy little inn. Soon, the local laird decided to get in on the act. In 1849 Lord Willoughby D'eresby, linked through marriage to the Dukes of Perth, commissioned a modern hotel of Baronial style on the site of the old inn. The Trossachs Hotel changed hands many times over the years, the last time in 1992. Following a multi-million pound refit, the renovated complex was re-opened by the Secretary of State, in September 1993, with its present name.

The guests are treated to the height of luxury. Tigh Mor is also environmentally friendly; energy conservation systems are in place and the sewage is bio-degraded through a series of reed-beds. A full range of facilities augments everything else that the Trossachs has to offer. A shop is open for an hour or so, morning and evening, a useful service both for locals and for walkers out to tackle Ben A'an.

Tigh Mor is definitely one of the jewels in the crown of the Trossachs.

Time

Time is something we all take for granted. Throughout the world it is accepted that there are 60 seconds in every minute, 60 minutes in an hour and 24 hours in a day. The fact that there are 365.242199 days in a calendar year is a minor problem, adequately dealt with by Pope Gregory's Leap Year calculation. It was the advent of clocks that standardised time keeping. Before, things were a little more flexible. A Roman day, which began at sunset, had twelve hours each of light and darkness – our winter nights had very long hours indeed!

There is, however, still a difference in time – the difference between this world and the other world. This can be illustrated by a story told by a seannachaidh at the ceilidh fire. *Two fiddle players, having played at a faery ball, returned to find their town completely changed. Having taken refuge in the church, the minister listened to their astonishing adventure – as the two young men began to visibly grow older by the minute. At the very moment the story was finished, the first rays of the newly risen sun slanted into the church, and the men crumbled instantly to dust – like a macabre egg timer.* They left behind the two fiddles, two purses full of gold and the story that had kept them away more than a hundred years. And there are many more such time-wrenched tales.

Not everyone who enters the faery realm suffers a time penalty. A young boy, brought up on one of the townships at the top end of Strathard, seemed to be able to visit the Little People without any problems – time and time again. He spoke of untold wealth in the Underworld – everything was either lined with or made from pure gold. He eventually succumbed to temptation, and never saw the faeries again.

The boy grew up to become an archbishop in the Episcopal Church. If you cannot believe the word of an archbishop, whose word can you believe?

Trossachs

The Trossachs is one of the most famous places in Scotland. Most people have heard of the Trossachs, even if they are not quite sure where it is exactly. Even locally there is confusion – where or what is the Trossachs? The Gaelic word *Troisichean* has been derived from the older Brythonic *tros*, meaning across or a cross over. So, Trossachs is a small, transverse glen that joins two larger glens. This Trossachs is just under a mile long, linking Loch Katrine with Loch Achray, and about half a mile wide. This small area, in the hands of the Tourist Board, has grown ever larger and now seems to include everywhere between Glasgow, Edinburgh, Perth and Oban!

There is a great deal of history locked into the Trossachs, an area that used to be so difficult to get to – and so easy to defend. Offshore crannogs and hilltop forts are testament to those turbulent times, and ancient place-names still speak of the past. Gartnait was a local chief who fought against the Irish invaders – the Scots – and is ever remembered by the Strath Gartney that cradles Loch Katrine. The era of the clans saw the MacGregors entrenched in Glen Gyle, the birthplace of Rob Roy. Those days are all long gone – but the stories linger on.

Many artists and writers have found inspiration in the Trossachs. There will hardly be an art gallery anywhere that does not have a scene of Loch Katrine. The magical light that plays across the landscape still has painters and photographers holding their breath. Images of the Trossachs, drawn up in words, have enthralled generations of readers. Besides Sir Walter Scott, many well known authors have taken storylines, characters and background from this wonderful place. Jules Verne set one of his adventures, *Les Indes noires* (The Underground City), in a community far below Loch Katrine. And then there were the poets – too numerous to count.

Tulloch

Tulloch is on the north shore of Loch Voil, a mile west of the village of Balquhidder, land once held by Clan Gregor. A small cave, frequently used by Rob Roy to elude his enemies, is hidden in the hillside above the farm. In the immediate aftermath of the '45 rising, Tulloch was one of the Balquhidder farms torched by government troops. Only the intervention of Rob Roy's son, Ranald, prevented an instant and bloody response. Eventually, compensation amounting to £157.12.8d was paid for the damage.

Tulach means a hillock, often one standing in marshy ground, as was the case here. The land has been greatly improved, especially during the time of David Carnegie, who bought Stronvar Estate in 1849. An intensive programme of drainage and pasture improvement was carried out. Carnegie acquired Tulloch and made it his Home Farm, bringing to an end the long tenure of the MacGregors. Above the farm, amongst the trees, the new laird planted rhododendrons and azaleas to resemble the shapes of Loch Viol and Loch Doine.

The last time that the loch froze to any great depth, a curling bonspiel was held at Tulloch, the short winter day floodlit by tractor headlights. One more end and yet another dram! People are welcome to walk through the Forestry Commission plantation on Tulloch hill. But look out for the ghostly hunter carrying a musket, accompanied by a brace of deerhounds – and, although not seen for many years, keep your eyes open for the elusive water beast of Loch Voil; you may just be lucky.

Tyndrum

The Statistical Account of 1796 gives only two villages in the parish of Killin; Killin itself, and the 200 strong mining community of Clifton. Immediately east of Clifton stood an inn known as Taigh an Druim, meaning 'the House on the Ridge'. With the military road from Stirling to Fort William being upgraded by the Turnpike

Acts of the 1820s, Tyndrum, with its new spelling, began to develop. Encircled by Corbetts, Munros, rivers and lochs, Tyndrum became a well known climbing, fishing and touring centre – especially for those seeking winter thrills. Situated in Strath Fillan, at 800 ft/247 m, Tyndrum is the highest settlement in the Loch Lomond and Trossachs National Park.

The peak of Ben Lui, from which the Fillan Water flows, is usually given as 'the Hill of (Deer) Calves'. It just may, however, derive from *luaidh* – lead. The lead mining on Meall Odhar was speculative at best but, by 1845, was enjoying quite a boom. German miners were brought in to augment the local force, a large crushing mill was built, and a railway system laid. Now, only a few shafts remain on the hillside, dark, dank and very slippery. In 1428, it was silver that was being taken out of the Royal Mine at Tyndrum. The 20th century saw more prospecting. It was hardly the Klondyke, but there was gold in the hills.

Here, at Dalrigh, Bruce was attacked by the MacDougalls of Lorne. A brooch, torn off the king's cloak, is still held by the clan. As Bruce and his men beat a hasty retreat, much of their armour and many weapons were hastily discarded in a small loch, Lochan nan Arm. Yet another setback on the long, long road to Bannockburn.

U

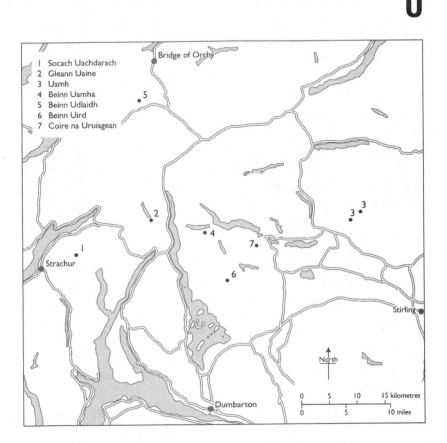

1 Socach Uachdarach
2 Gleann Uaine
3 Uamh
4 Beinn Uamha
5 Beinn Udlaidh
6 Beinn Uird
7 Coire na Uruisgean

Bridge of Orchy

Strachur

Stirling

North

Dumbarton

0   5   10   15 kilometres
0   5   10 miles

Socach Uachdarach

Socach means a pert female, a breast; *uachdarach* is upper or higher. There is no beating about the bush with this place name. Socach Uachdarach stands proud, north east of Strachur. The ground touches 1,896 ft/578 m and, from these slopes, the headwaters of the River Cur begin to flow towards Loch Eck. Conifer trees cup Socach Uachdarach like a piece of green lingerie. With the benefit of forestry roads, access from Strachur to this shapely hill is straightforward,

191

provided you can find the right track. The forest road along the south side of the river is best, leading to Upper Succoth and beyond.

Once clear of the trees the views open up; hills, glens, sea and sky... and then more trees. From here, most of Scotland seems to have been planted into one enormous forest. To the north east, even Hell's Glen lies deep in trees. Known to the Gael as Gleann Beag, it was at one time lit from end to end with the fires of charcoal burners – fuel for iron smelting. How I would love to bring back those fires! Far too much of this beautiful country is buried.

However, there is still a great deal to enjoy. A complete traverse of Socach Uachdarach can be made, either into Hell's Glen or to Loch Fyne.

Gleann Uaine

Gleann Uaine, 'Green Valley', in the Arrochar Alps, is a place that raises goose bumps on your arms and makes the hairs on the back of your neck stand up. Gleann Uaine runs north, dropping down from the high pass (1,640 ft/500 m) between the Munro peaks of Ben Vane and Beinn Ime. The meeting point of the glens is called Lag Uaine, a 'Green Hollow', where Glen Coiregrogain and Gleann Leacann Shellach disgorge hardy Munro baggers from Inveruglas and Succoth.

The most direct route to Gleann Uaine is from Butterbridge, west of the Rest and be Thankful. A track pushes north into the hills; it was once considered as an alternative to the road that was eventually constructed. Two miles up the Kinglas Water, the mouth of Gleann Uaine is guarded by an ancient dwelling and sheep fank, a place known as Abyssinia. The name derives from the Greek word for deep or bottomless – a place in the bowels of the earth.

This was the natural fortress of the wild MacFarlanes, gathering for their sprees at Loch Sloy and hiding the cattle so skilfully lifted in the fastness of Gleann Uaine. Once out of sight in the heart of these Alps, the rightful owners of the beasts were unlikely ever to see them again.

Amongst the numerous hill lochans is one whose waters are indelibly green. Here, long ago, the faeries produced and dyed their cloth. On one occasion, almost taken unawares by human beings, the Little People only had enough time to conceal the dye pot in the lochan before making themselves scarce. This is Lochan Uaine, green from the dye, easy enough to find once but, so I am told, much more difficult to locate a second time!

Uamhs

A *uamh*, generally pronounced as *weem*, is a cave – and there are lots of them. Two feature in this piece: Uamh Mhor (*weem vore*), 'the Big Cave', and Uamh Bheag (*weem beg*), 'the Little Cave', which give their names to neighbouring hilltops near Callander. Confusingly, Uamh Mhor, at 1,968 ft/600 m, is lower than Uamh Bheag (2,181 ft/664 m). The view from both these summits is south west to Callander and south east, over the Braes of Doune, towards Stirling. Immediately north are the Highlands.

The Big Cave is not really a cave at all, just a hollow beneath a very large boulder. Legend tells that it was once home to one of the giants who roamed these ancient hills. Later it became the lair of robbers, a desperate band whose reign of terror was brought to an end only 40 years before the time of Sir Walter Scott. Now the cave stands empty, except for a very fine echo. From solid rock, on the south east flank of this twin headed hill, flows a strong spring of water. This is the source of the Garvald Burn.

This is an area of early human settlement. Unfortunately, much of the evidence has been obliterated by agriculture and peat encroachment. However, on the higher ground, some Stone Age monuments still survive. A Neolithic round cairn with a chamber has been identified on Uamh Bheag, one of several in this area.

There is a good approach to these hills from Callander, via Meall Leathan Dhail, and several alternatives across the Braes of Doune. The more adventurous could tackle Uamh Bheag and Mhor from the Crieff side, starting in lovely Glen Artney.

Beinn Uamha

Beinn Uamha (1,955 ft/596 m) is a little known hill, lost amongst the mountains and hidden by the furthest reaches of the Loch Ard Forest. However, the trees are gradually being stripped away, once more revealing the beautiful underlying landscape. Although the highest hill on the south shore of Loch Arklet, the eye is first captured by the mountain sweep to the north – and then by the sheer grandeur of the Arrochar Alps against the western sky. Poor Beinn Uamha is seldom noticed. Pronounced *ooa* or *oova*, either this is 'the Hill of the Cavern' or it is named for an ancient chieftain.

Everyone should climb Beinn Uamha at least once in their lifetime. It will be an unforgettable experience. All around, mountains and glens, water and sky... so much sky. The light just keeps changing, never the same from one moment to the next, like an ever moving kaleidoscope. The view from the head of Loch Arklet must be one of the most frequently photographed in the whole of Scotland. Many cars and buses stop to let the passengers take in the scene. Just imagine what it must look like from another 1,300 ft!

There are a few handy parking spaces alongside the B829, but *not* in any of the small passing places, which are extremely limited in number. The simplest way to get to Beinn Uamha is to follow the pylon line that crosses the top of Strathard. The cables stretch up from Loch Katrine, across the single-track road, and head in the direction of Ben Lomond. At the sixth pylon you meet the nascent River Forth and should see your way to the summit.

Between pylons four and five, there is a hidden delight – Lochan Mhaim nan Carn. During the summer this is the haunt of a pair of red-throated divers. It is good for fishing, too.

Beinn Udlaidh

The flat, stony summit of Beinn Udlaidh (2,755 ft/840 m) is only three miles from Tyndrum. The mountain broods over the A85 as it runs through Glen Lochy. Pronounced *ootly*, the name means dark or gloomy. In tandem with neighbouring Beinn Bhreac-laith, 'the Speckled Grey Hill', Beinn Udlaidh offers a good hill walking excursion. Extensive tree planting over the lower slopes has severely restricted access, so good use has to be made of the few remaining gaps.

The shortest route begins from Arinabea, a farm steading alongside the A85. A tumbling burn provides a break through the unnatural forest, leading to open ground and a coll between the two hills. Above the tree line the landscape is strewn with rock and boulders and a multitude of tiny lochans reflects the light. The plateau of Udlaidh lies to the west, with stunning views of mountain and muirland, water and woodland – and sky.

For a longer and much more interesting climb, start from the back door in Glen Orchy. From Invergaunan, on the B8074, follow the Allt Ghamhnain upstream. Bear westward towards the north ridge of Beinn Udlaidh and a spectacular band of white quartz. Clearly visible for many miles, this volcanic intrusion crosses the entire ridge and runs into the steep cliffs of Coire Daimh, at the north west flank of the beinn.

There are good bus and train services to Tyndrum and Bridge of Orchy, both within easy walking distance of Beinn Udlaidh.

Beinn Uird

Beinn Uird rises to 1,958 ft/597 m, behind Rowardennan, on the east side of Loch Lomond. Like many Gaelic words beginning with the letter *U*, rendition into English is a little bit tricky. Uird should sound something like *oursht*. Beinn Uird means 'the Hill of Hammering', from *ord* – a hammer. It was on this hill, a long time ago, that Finn McCoul's giant smiths forged mighty weapons for his warrior people. Many great battles were fought by Finn and his men, their bravery unmatched and their swords never bettered.

The long approach to Beinn Uird is from Gleann Dubh, 'the Secret Valley' hidden between Aberfoyle and the east side of Ben

Lomond. A forestry road runs the entire length of this glen – if you can find the way in. It was from this stronghold that Finn would set out to wage war or hunt down the finest stags. Trees now cover the ground where giants once roamed and people once farmed. Gleann Dubh is eerily quiet. The giants now sleep deep underground, and two hundred years ago the people went away to Canada. Now it is the men from the Forestry Commission who hunt the deer – leaving hardly a stag to roar into the autumn nights.

A track towards the headwater of Bruach Caorainn and the summit of Beinn Uird passes a well-preserved township. Ahead, rising out of the forest, is Creag na h'Ulaidhe – 'the Rock or Cliff of Treasure' – a name with a dark origin. *Ula(dh)* is a mound or monument over a grave, from which treasure was presumably looted.

Alternative descents from Beinn Uird are either to Rowardennan, or via Blairvockie Farm to the road at Loch Lomondside.

Underworld

Most of us are well aware of the world around about, we are familiar with the sky above, have knowledge of the ground beneath our feet. But what goes on below, down in the Underworld, remains a mystery to most mortals. And that is the way they want it to stay – it is better not knowing. However, throughout history, people have come up with strange tales of another place, far different from anything previously experienced.

Such stories can be found in many parts of the world, curiously consistent in their content. Scottish folklore has a rich vein of tales from the Underworld, especially within the area of Scotland's first National Park. Some never return from their visits there. If you would like to explore the Underworld for yourself, try walking seven times anti-clockwise round a faerie hill at sunrise on May Day. When the door opens, go in if you dare!

Coire na Uruisgean

Coire na Uruisgean, often translated as 'Goblins' Cave', is on the south shore of Loch Katrine, under the protective bulwark of Ben Venue. This strange place, with its mysterious inhabitants, has long been made famous through the writings of popular authors. In spite of the stories of Sir Walter Scott, Jules Verne and many others, there are no goblins – and there is no cave. The Uruisgean did exist, but they were certainly not 'goblins'.

The Celts, who arrived 2,500 years ago, had a society with a strict cast system. Their religious leaders were known as druids, warrior-priests who definitely led from the front. When the Romans arrived they greatly feared the druids and persecuted them mercilessly. From this time, and with the introduction of Christianity, the druids were continuously under pressure from a changing world. The last enclave of these people was an inaccessible corrie, tucked away above the south shore of Loch Katrine.

Here they survived, and continued to be consulted by those who had need of their great powers. The druids, however, had to protect themselves from an increasingly hostile world. Their first line of defence was to spread strange stories, designed to keep the outside world at bay. Then they began to cultivate a frightening appearance – half animal, half man. By mingling with the local population of wild goats, nobody knew whether these Uruisgean really existed or not. A local MacDonald, who claimed to have shot the last goat on Ben Venue, said that as the very last animal tumbled off a high rocky ledge to meet its maker, it cried out in a strange language.

The easiest and safest way to see Coire na Uruisgean is from the decks of the ss *Sir Walter Scott*.

V

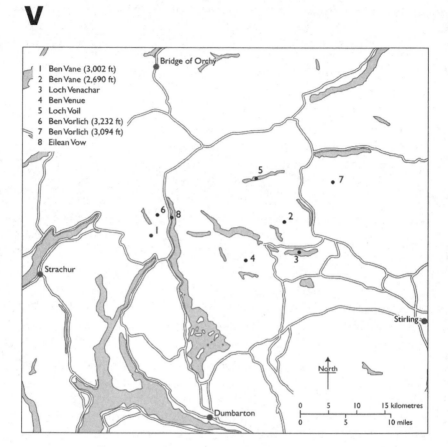

1 Ben Vane (3,002 ft)
2 Ben Vane (2,690 ft)
3 Loch Venachar
4 Ben Venue
5 Loch Voil
6 Ben Vorlich (3,232 ft)
7 Ben Vorlich (3,094 ft)
8 Eilean Vow

Ben Vane

The letter *v* only appears in Scottish place names when borrowed from Old Norse or through a peculiarity of Gaelic grammar. An initial consonant is sometimes altered, *b-* to *bh-* or *m-* to *mh-*, both pronounced as *v*. Ben Vane (3,002 ft/915 m) takes its name from *mheadhoin* – middle hill – and is located at the very heart of the Arrochar Alps. Just to confuse the issue, the *dh* in *mheadhoin* is silent!

Ben Vane only makes it onto the list of 284 Munros by two feet. Of the 21 Munros within the Loch Lomond and Trossachs National Park, Ben Vane is certainly the steepest. The south face, above Allt Coiregrogain, rises 2,000 ft at an angle of almost 45 degrees – not the easiest way up! Ascent of Ben Vane is usually made from Inveruglas, on the A82. Parking is available to the north of the power station. Please, do not park at the foot of the Loch Sloy access road.

The Hydro Board road makes for an easy way into the hills, encouraging many more people to come and enjoy the wonderful scenery. Be prepared for the weather. This is an area of high rainfall – over 120 inches (3,050 mm) a year. It can be wet from above and soggy underfoot. Follow the track west beyond Coiregrogain Farm for about a mile. Then look for the path up the south east ridge of Ben Vane. Eventually the route threads its way through some rocky outcrops to the great views at the top.

Once across the Inveruglas Water, flowing from the dammed Loch Sloy, the roads and the pylons marking the progress of man quickly recede. Up on the high summits little has changed since the last Ice Age retreated, 10,000 years ago.

Ben Vane

Another Ben Vane (2,690 ft/820 m) is found in the Trossachs, to the north of Glen Finglas Reservoir. The name, in this case, means 'the White Hill', from Gaelic *bhan* – white, the colour of sun-bleached grass at the end of summer. This grass, known as purple moor grass, *Molinia coerulea*, is an important source of food for hill sheep, deer and a great deal of wildlife. It was the grazing of sheep, and the burning off of the remaining grass, that kept natural forest generation at bay, maintaining a man-made environment.

The centuries old track down Glen nam Meann, on the east side of Ben Vane, was an important route from the north towards Glasgow. This was a main thoroughfare for drovers, traders and a great many whisky smugglers. It is still a fine footpath to Balquhidder. Much of Ben Vane is owned by the Woodland Trust, which is restoring the natural forest. This will augment the few ancient trees that have withstood fire and grazing through the ages.

From the top of Ben Vane there is a fine view of the Finglas Reservoir, completed in 1965 to increase the capacity of Loch Katrine and generate hydroelectricity. This is a remarkable area for wildlife; animals and birds abound. It's pretty good for butterflies and moths, too. Look out for the large, brown, hairy caterpillar of the Northern Eggar. Feeding mostly on heather, it has a two-year life cycle before becoming a moth. This is also the haunt of the Scotch Argus butterfly, whose caterpillars eat the *Molinia*.

Loch Venachar

Loch Venachar is an expansion of the western headwaters of the Teith. The loch was enlarged during the second half of the 19th century, as part of the development by the Glasgow Water Authority. Large embankments were constructed, with a dam and sluices to raise the water level – now 280 ft/85 m above sea level – and control the outflow into the river. There is still a legal require- ment to release sufficient water to power the mills and factories that, long ago, drew their energy from the Teith.

The name Venachar may derive from Gaelic *bhana* – fair – and *choire* – hollow – describing a 'fair valley'. However, an older spelling gives Vennachar, from the Gaelic *Bheannchair*. In this case, *beann* is horn and *cor* means location or situation. This is a version dating back to 1375. Before flooding the valley, this long, narrow loch, which had a number of tributaries, is said to have resembled a cast antler. So, Loch Venachar probably translates better as 'the Antler Loch'.

Loch Venachar must be the most accessible in the land, com- pletely encircled by roads and footpaths. National Cycle Route 7 skirts the south shore, a beautiful and very level section. Here stands Invertrossachs House, frequented by Queen Victoria, now offering rather exclusive accommodation to its clientele. There are a couple of picnic sites and good car parking along the north shore. But walking is best; Callander and Aberfoyle are both within easy range.

There are many woodland walks to enjoy, but one area ought to be avoided – Coillebhroine, 'the Wood of Lamentation'. It was from this lochside field, many years ago, that 12 local children were carried to their doom by the kelpie of Loch Venachar. The meadow was never grazed again, and a fine stand of trees serve as a memorial to the lost souls.

Ben Venue

The meaning of Ben Venue is quite contentious but is probably indicative of its size, or lack of size. The Gaelic *Beinn Mheanbh* could simply translate as 'Small Mountain'. At 2,386 ft/727 m, Ben Venue falls 114 ft short of even making it onto the Corbett list. Never-the-less, the striking outline of Ben Venue imposes itself firmly on the Trossachs skyline and has been much lauded in poetry, prose and painting.

Best viewed from the decks of the ss *Sir Walter Scott*, sedately steaming past on the waters of Loch Katrine, or from the north shore road opposite, the mountain is simply magnificent. The summit looks down onto Bealach nam Bo, 'the Pass of the Cattle', the only route across this side of the ben. Further down is the steep, cauldron-shaped corrie filled with rocks and mounds, like fragments of an earlier world, known as the Goblins' Cave.

To get the best out of Ben Venue, make a complete traverse from Achray to Kinlochard. In the summer season this is possible by starting at Kinlochard and catching the postbus to Stonachlachar pier, and then boarding the steamer to the Trossachs. By crossing the dam at the east end of Loch Katrine, you pick up the footpath heading westwards. Leave the path where it turns inland and climb through the obvious gully straight ahead. Keep going anti-clockwise, around the shoulder of Ben Venue. On meeting the well-eroded track up from the south side, it is right to Kinlochard and left to the twin tops. The first summit, without the trig point, is actually the higher of the two.

Since Scottish Water decided to stop farming their land and cleared off the sheep, walking over these beautiful hills has become much more difficult, but it is well worth the effort.

Loch Voil

Beautiful Loch Voil sits snugly in the narrow glen of Balquhidder, less than half a mile wide and running more than three miles towards the setting sun. The view from the lofty crag above Balquhidder church, overlooking Loch Voil and neighbouring Loch Doine, is simply magnificent. Beyond, deep in the recess of the glen, is Inverlochlarig Beag, where Rob Roy died in December 1734.

The influence of the old Brythonic dialect can be found in the earlier pronunciation of *Balwhither*, as found in the language of the Welsh. In this case, the first letter of Voil would come from a single *f* rendered in speech as a *v*. *Foil* translates as a den or lurking place – a very apt description indeed. In fact, this was the very last truly lawless area in Scotland, and therefore a favourite lurking place for outlaws and broken men.

Well sheltered by the mountains, every fertile acre proved to be so productive that James IV gave these lands to his Welsh queen, Margaret Tudor. The lands may have been owned by powerful lords, but actual control lay with the local clans; the Stewarts, MacLarens and above all, MacGregors. Clan Gregor maintained a stronghold on an ancient crannog, just off the south shore at the east end of Loch Voil. If this was not enough to protect the residents, stories of a serpent-like monster inhabiting the loch were sure to inhibit unwanted visitors.

To the south is the mouth of Glen Buckie and an excellent walk through the hills to Brig o' Turk. Eastwards flows the River Balvaig, meandering into Strathyre, eventually feeding into the waters of the Teith.

Ben Vorlich

There are two mountains of this name, separated by only 21 miles east to west, and both Munros. The eastern sentinel (3,232 ft/985 m) stands on the edge of the Highlands, overlooking Loch Earn. Gazing north from the Forth Valley, the pointed peak of this Ben Vorlich sits astride one of a pair of parallel ridges running away to the north west. The flatter, left hand neighbour is Stuc a'Chroin and between them they make up one of the conspicuous features of the northern skyline.

The name Vorlich has given rise to much speculation. It is thought by some to derive from Gaelic *balg* – a (sea) bay or bag, or a slang form of belly. The Latin form is *balga* – a pouch or bulge. Others have suggested that it is a personal name. There was a fiendish Celtic weapon, only ever used by the greatest of warriors, known as the *gae-bholg* – belly spear – which was propelled by the foot to devastating effect. Dim stories exist of an ancient chieftain, remembered by his weapon of choice, who held lands between the two mountains that carry his name, Vorlich.

Access to Ben Vorlich from the north was somewhat restricted by the devastation inflicted by the summer storms of 2004 and repairs to the south Loch Earnside road have still to be completed. So no hurry there, then. Taking the same path from the Callander end, along the Kelty Water, is a much longer hike. An alternative route is to start from Ardchullarie More, at the side of Loch Lubnaig, in Strathyre, and approach Ben Vorlich through Glen Ample.

Ben Vorlich

The second Ben Vorlich (3,094 ft/943 m) is the most northerly summit of the Arrochar Alps, and by far the most popular. There are so many ways to the top of Ben Vorlich, overlooking the northern waters of Loch Lomond, that it has managed to avoid the usual problem of having a single, greatly eroded footpath. The ben is a long crescent, north to south, with a steep, craggy western flank falling away towards Loch Sloy. The dark waters lie deep and still, waiting to be unleashed into hydroelectric power.

A tunnel, 15 ft 4 inches in diameter, two miles (3.2 km) in length, passes through the heart of Ben Vorlich. Emerging at the 650 ft/200 m contour, four steel pipes plunge down the hillside to the power station. Each pipe is almost 7 ft/2 m in diameter, and they have been well anchored by concrete blocks weighing up to 3,600 tons (3,657 tonnes). The tunnel was completed in April 1949 and the generators first turned the following February. On 18 October 1950, Queen Elizabeth formally threw the switches to feed power into the National Grid. The pipes are still a blot on the landscape.

The best route to the top of Ben Vorlich is from Stuckendroin, south of Ardlui station. Take the second pass under the West Highland Railway and head south west up the heather slopes, towards the ridge. Cross the Little Hills, several knolls and a couple of small tops, and head down into a col and upwards once more to the summit – and breathtaking views. No wonder Ben Vorlich is so popular.

Eilean Vow

Eilean Vow stands alone, the most northerly island of Loch Lomond. Sometimes referred to as Island 1 Vow, the tree-clad acre is situated mid-channel, between Ben Vorlich to the west and the towering east bank reaching up to Beinn a'Choin. Two miles from the head of the loch, Eilean Vow is steeped in history, folklore and legend. Wordsworth even penned some verses about one of the inhabitants in his poem, 'The Brownie's Cell'.

The meaning of the name is usually given as 'Island of the Cow', from the Gaelic *Eilean a'Bho*. The local MacFarlanes, ensconced on the west of the loch, were renowned cattle rustlers. Eilean Vow was certainly one of their refuges. However, there are earlier references, including a Gaelic poem of 1507, interpreting the name as 'Island of the Bow', from *Eilean a'Bhealaich*. Bows would have been much used in these parts.

Another option is taken from *Elan Vanow*, *Eilean Bhannaomh*, translated as 'Island of Holy Women'. There are certainly ancient ruins, later fortified by the warlike MacFarlanes, now shrouded in deep foliage. But there are very early flowering daffodils on the island, coming into bloom before any others in this locality. These were said to have been planted long ago, to celebrate Easter – blooming in time for the festival each year, no matter how early it fell. So the holy women cannot be completely discounted.

Eilean Vow is claimed to be uninhabited. Not so. The little island is the haunt of countless small, dark, furry animals – voles. Hundreds of them, and seemingly quite unafraid of man. They are even mentioned in a 9th century poem, found in the Book of Lismore.

W

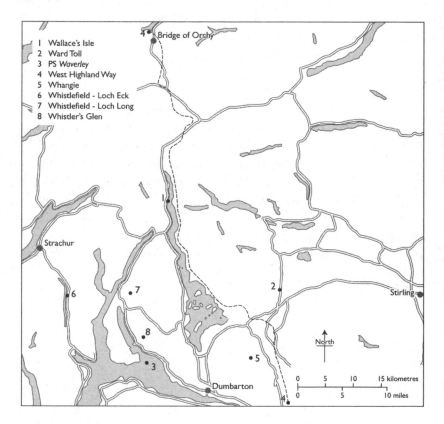

1 Wallace's Isle
2 Ward Toll
3 PS *Waverley*
4 West Highland Way
5 Whangie
6 Whistlefield - Loch Eck
7 Whistlefield - Loch Long
8 Whistler's Glen

Wallace's Isle

There has only ever been one name recorded for the low, flat, tree covered island that lies in the mouth of Inveruglas Water – Wallace's Isle. This is the only island on the whole of Loch Lomond without any alternative appellation. As this name can be traced back over centuries, it can be assumed that it does indeed have direct links with Scotland's great hero, William Wallace. Seven hundred years is a long time to remain unchanged.

It is believed on the lochside that Wallace used this island as a guerrilla base during his insurgency against Edward Longshanks. Victorious at the Battle of Stirling Bridge in September 1297, Wallace laid waste to the north of England. This brought Edward I back to Scotland with a large force and Wallace was defeated at Falkirk, but only just. Until his betrayal by John Stewart, in 1305, the struggle continued – much of it supposedly launched out of this Highland retreat. The fastness of this place was quite forbidding.

Wallace's Isle is well hidden from the road, tucked in behind the holiday park. The island is so close to the surrounding shores that the roots of some of the alder trees must easily reach the mainland. The best way to see Wallace's Isle is to cruise up the loch from Tarbet. The island lies due west of Inversnaid, immediately opposite the Duke of Montrose's old hunting lodge, up on the hillside and now the Inversnaid Photography Centre.

There is no evidence that Wallace was ever on the isle, but there is nothing to say that he was not.

Ward Toll

Ward Toll is situated four miles south of Aberfoyle, on the A81, overlooking the edge of Flanders Moss and the Highlands beyond. Best known for the plant nursery, Ward Toll is a place most people drive past, unless stopping for some garden requirements, a visit to the farm shop or a bite to eat. At one time everybody stopped at the tollhouse to pay their dues, before proceeding on their way. The name, however, predates the age of any road building.

Dr Johnson noted on his Scottish tour that, in places, there would be a herdsman who knew all the cattle. His station on the hill allowed him to drive any straying beasts back to their own ground. The English word for this duty is watch or ward, from Old English, weard; Old Norman French has *warde*. From the north facing slopes of Ward Toll, any *buachaille* or herdsman could keep a safe eye on his charges and ward them from cattle thieves.

The Ward Burn flows north east, towards the low-lying moss. In geological terms, this is land over which the North Sea recently ebbed and flowed. Even in Roman times it was a forbidding morass, seemingly impassable. In inimitable style, the Romans built a road across the quaking bog, with the usual attendant forts. The earthwork of one of these can clearly be seen, just to the east of the A81. Long ago the stone was removed by William MacFarlane, to build himself a farmhouse at Freuchan, Gartmore.

The views from the little coffee shop, along the Highland boundary and right down the Forth Valley, are in themselves a reason to stop a while at Ward Toll.

PS Waverley

There can be few sights more stirring than that of the Paddle Steamer *Waverley* churning her way through the waters of the Clyde. It is sure to get the salt in our veins pumping just that much faster, in anticipation of a cruise 'doon the watter'. She was commissioned in 1945 to replace her predecessor of the same name, bombed into oblivion during the Dunkerque evacuation. Like all other paddle steamers, she had been called up to serve as a minesweeper. Fast, manoeuvrable and shallow draughted, they were ideal for the job.

The keel of the new *Waverley* was laid in December 1945 and she was ready to launch on 2 October the following year. Sent to be fitted-out early in 1947, PS *Waverley* soon took up station at her base at Craigendoran. But the Age of Steam was coming to an end, as the motorcar and air travel were beginning to take people elsewhere. All around the coast, steam ships were scrapped and piers fell into disrepair. Before long, the *Waverley* was the last ocean going paddle steamer in the whole world.

In 1974, on the point of being consigned to the breakers' yard, the vessel was acquired by new owners, for the princely price of £1. The Waverley Steam Navigation Company has transformed the old ship, now well past her 50th anniversary. New paddle wheels, a modern boiler and the most up to date electronic equipment all comply with the stringent, 21st century regulations. Many years of hard work by a small group of dedicated people have ensured that future generations will still be able to cruise along the Clyde under steam.

West Highland Way

In 1968 the Countryside Commission for Scotland set the wheels in motion to establish long-distance footpaths. The proposal for a West Highland Way was approved by the Secretary of State in September 1974, conceived as a route between Glasgow and Fort William. The Countryside Commission and the Local Authorities along this 95-mile footpath were given considerable support in their efforts to make the plan a reality. Many wet sections were cleared and drained, bridges built, and wooden way markers with thistle motifs put in place.

The West Highland Way was officially opened by the Earl of Mansfield on 6 October 1980. Although Milngavie is recognised as the southern point of the Way, it is possible to start from the heart of the city, at the Botanic Gardens. North from Milngavie, the West Highland Way passes through 25 places featured in this book, as well as traversing the entire east bank of Loch Lomond. These first 57 miles/92 km will take the walker into a landscape of wildness and beauty unmatched anywhere else in Europe.

The main problem that walkers face is water – especially the water underfoot. Good boots, already well broken in, are essential. A useful tip, from a hill shepherd, is to line your boots with a good layer of wool. Thankfully, there are services that will transport baggage to the next port of call, leaving you to catch up with it – eventually. There are good hotels and comfy bed and breakfasts along the Way, with a Youth Hostel at Rowardennan and another at Crianlarich. Bunkhouses, at Inversnaid and Bridge of Orchy, provide good, economy-class accommodation.

For more than a quarter of a century, the West Highland Way has provided the opportunity for countless people to tackle its challenges. Whether accomplished in short sections or completed in one go, 95 miles is a long way to walk.

Whangie

The Whangie is an enormous rent found in the grey, storm-beaten rocks, exposed on the north face of Auchineden Hill. Overlooking Stockiemuir, the chasm is between three and 10 ft wide, 50 ft deep, and an impressive 346 ft long. The Whangie is said to have been made by Old Nick himself. The Devil had dropped in to meet a coven of his followers, and became so aroused and excited by them that his tail swished out of control. One blow from that tail was enough to split the bedrock. In Scots parlance, that was a whangie.

From the earliest days of mountaineering, this Whangie has been a Mecca for enthusiasts of the sport. Not only is the Whangie said to present almost every climbing difficulty known to man, it is only ten miles from the centre of Glasgow. The rock is basalt, formed from lava. During a period of volcanic activity, the eruption of molten rock was preceded by the formation of a layer of tuff – small, hard lumps of lava mixed with ash. Any later rock laid over tuff is inherently unstable, slowly sliding away to produce one Whangie after another. The present Whangie looks pretty precarious.

Throughout history the Whangie has proved to be a useful hiding place. Stolen cattle could be kept from view and hunted men would remain unseen in the deep recess. The freshwater spring, just below the rocks, would have been invaluable. You will find the water as thirst quenching today, after walking across from the Queen's View car park or taking the longer route from Carbeth Inn. And never mind the climbing – the views are great.

Whistlefield

The first of two Whistlefields in the area of the Loch Lomond and Trossachs National Park is situated on the A815, seven miles south of Strachur. Centred on the inn, dating from 1663, Whistlefield also has waterside holiday lodges offering panoramic views of Loch Eck and the surrounding valley. A ferry used to ply the narrow stretch of water, summoned by a whistle from the opposite bank – hence the name Whistlefield.

Whistlefield looks west across the deep, narrow glen, gouged out by passing glaciers grinding their way towards the south. At one time open to the sea, Loch Eck is now a fresh water body, fed by the River Cur flowing in from the north. Countless burns pour down the steep mountainsides before vanishing beneath the hemline of conifers, which seemingly encircles the loch. The deepest water lies just offshore, measured at over 100 ft.

The blanket of 20th century trees, part of the Argyll Forest Park, has brought hidden benefits. There are miles and miles of well-built forestry roads on both sides of the loch. A cycle route has been developed through to Glen Branter and Glen Shellish. From Whistlefield it is possible to take the picturesque little road over the hill to Glen Finnart and Loch Long. The less adventurous can simply relax at the picnic site on the shore of Loch Eck and take in the scenery.

West Coast Motors operate bus services between Dunoon and Inveraray or Carrick Castle, both via Whistlefield.

The second Whistefield in the National Park is wonderfully positioned – it stands high on a ridge, one mile north of Garelochhead, and looks west over Loch Long and into the mouth of Loch Goil. Unfortunately, rampant roadside tree generation has greatly reduced the all-round visibility. This tiny community is situated at a major crossroads, complete with roundabout, on the A814. Running west and then south is the new road to Coulport, still under military control. The road known as Whistlefield Brae, built by the Duke of Argyll, drops down to the Gareloch.

The West Highland Railway passes through Whistlefield, though the station closed in 1964. For many years this hamlet was a popular interchange for passengers enjoying the rail and ferry boat tours of the area. Locally landed fish was collected by the passenger trains and transported, absolutely fresh, to southern destinations. During the war years, German prisoners were carried to and from their labours at the Loch Sloy hydroelectric scheme by these trains. The campsite is now a picnic area and viewpoint – pity about the screen of trees.

Whistling has long been used as a means of communication, as illustrated by shepherds working with their dogs. From Whistlefield it would certainly be possible to make contact across the water with Argyll's Bowling Green, Buaile na Greine, meaning 'the Sunny Cattle Fold'. But here a whistle was more likely to be employed as an early warning to the men working at the illicit stills. A great deal of moonshine came out of these hills, shipped away under cover of darkness to a very thirsty world beyond.

Whistler's Glen

Sir Walter Scott mentions Whistler's Glen in *Heart of Midlothian*. It takes its name from the curlew calls made to warn whisky makers that the Excise Men were approaching. Scotland's great novelist gleaned many plots, story lines and characters from north of the Highland Line, and he found all three in abundance in this glen, hidden on the east side of the Gare Loch. Sir Walter may well have orchestrated the Scottish visit of King George VI, but it was the Duke of Argyll who supplied the whisky, taken from this glen.

Tucked away behind the little village of Rhu, shrouded by trees, the Ordnance Survey marks Whistler's Glen as Aldownick Glen. In Gaelic, that would be *Allt Donnag* – 'the Stream of the Young Ling' (heather). Locally, this has become the Aldonaig Burn. From its main spring, high on Tom na h-Airigh, the water runs over open grass and heather moorland before disappearing into a conifer plantation. On emerging from the trees, the burn is captured to fill a series of three small reservoirs. After this, the water really gets to work, producing a natural wonder.

For more than half a mile the burn has sliced a deep, steep-sided gorge through the ancient bedrock, exposing aeons of geology. Tall native trees add to the seclusion. Faint outlines of old stone walls hint at earlier activity. Wood there is aplenty – and soft, peaty water, ideal for the stillman's needs. Many a pair of hands would have guddled trout out of a series of pools, seemingly created for this very purpose. The Aldonaig Burn has yet one more trick, becoming a feature in several private gardens before reaching the sea.

This place is so secret that it only seems to be visited by the annual run of sea trout returning to breed. Whistler's Glen was, however, bombed by the Germans during World War II, the craters remaining to the present day. What could they have been after?

X

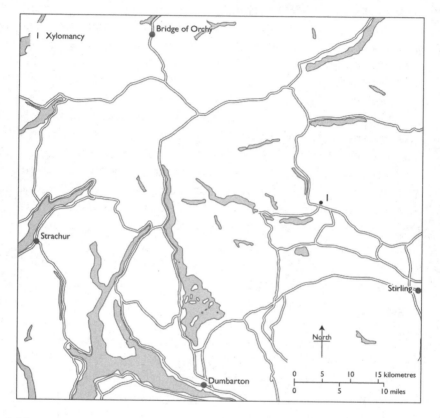

X

X is the 24th letter and 19th consonant of the English alphabet. X is also used to denote an algebraic variable, a choice on a ballot paper, a wrong answer, a kiss at the bottom of a letter and the Roman numeral for ten. But in Scotland it is instantly recognised as the symbol of St Andrew, patron saint of this ancient kingdom – the shape of the cross upon which the apostle was put to death in 60 AD.

The story of Andrew, fisherman of Galilee, is as enthralling now as it always was. The place of execution was Patras, in south west Greece, and the bones of the apostle would have been dispersed locally as sacred relics and good luck charms. Three hundred years later, the Roman Empire found itself riven from within by power struggles and attacked from without by barbarian hordes – including the North Britons. The old bones of St Andrew needed to be taken to a safer place.

It is claimed that a monk called Regulus, translated into English as Rule, brought the relics to the East Neuk of Fife, a safe haven in those troubled times. Nothing much then happened until the year 761, when Athelstane of Northumbria marched north. As a small army of Picts and Scots prepared to engage a much larger force of Angles and Saxons about 17 miles east of Edinburgh, white clouds formed the cross of St Andrew against the blue sky – and a nation's flag was born.

The Saltire is the oldest national flag in the world.

XXX

X is not a letter of the Celtic alphabets but would have been known to the learned men who had understanding of Greek. It would seem that our ancestors were not much interested in the written word, all knowledge being committed to memory by the all powerful druids. This degree of learning and knowledge scared the Romans, more so than any show of military might.

Celtic druids travelled widely, right across Europe and as far as Tibet, even to China. They would have returned with many new ideas and greatly enhanced skills. Three thousand years ago the Greeks discovered the secrets of fermentation, turning simple grape and cereal juices into something much more exciting. The druids then took this process a step further – concentrating the alcohol by distillation and producing spirit.

The druids identified this wonderful creation by borrowing the letter x from the Greek alphabet. This was very significant; x in Greek is the first letter of Christ's name. How apt to use the initial of the Way of Life to signify the Water of Life! With x established as the mark for spirit, xx indicated stronger spirit and xxx the strongest of all. Later, brewers adopted the same system to indicate the strength of their ale. However, xxxx means nothing at all – it is just an advertising gimmick.

Xanthoria

Xanthoria parientina is something that most people have noticed but few will be able to name. It is a bright yellow lichen found growing on bare rock, especially close to the sea. A lichen is a complex association of two plants, a fungus and an alga, living and working together as one complex organism. Lichens play an important role in primary plant colonisation, becoming established where few other species could live. They are also good indicators of air quality.

In days gone by xanthoria was put to many uses. As a remedy it could be taken by mouth, or applied externally. By itself, or in combination with other herbs and plant extracts, xanthoria was believed to relieve sickness and promote healing. Even today there are practitioners who hold on to these old secrets. They could probably save the National Health Service a great deal of money.

Xanthoria is still used to dye white wool by those who can be bothered to go out and collect it. The lichen has to be painstakingly scraped off rocks and boulders. Weight for weight there must be as much xanthoria as wool. That is a lot of scraping! However, xanthoria produces a dye-fast colour without the need of a fixing agent – in this case, the agent would be an expensive burnished 9 ct gold.

Xanthoria, along with other lichens, grow very slowly and reproduce with difficulty. They should be treated with great care. Xanthoria can brighten up even the dullest day at the seaside, and is found in many places throughout the National Park.

Xenoliths

From the Greek for foreign rock, xenoliths are pieces of bedrock that have been torn off and trapped inside solidified lava. The geology of Loch Lomond and the surrounding landscape can be traced back more than 600 million years. The countryside is being continuously altered by wind, rain, frost, water erosion, and the occasional small earthquake. Volcanic activity also played a part once, though hopefully it is long extinct.

The northern reaches of Loch Lomond have cut deeply into ancient metamorphic rock; sedimentary formations altered by heat and pressure and thrust up into a great mountain range. At the broader, shallower southern end of the loch, a chain of tree covered islands marks the line of the Highland Boundary Fault. This separates the ancient geology of the Highlands from the younger and softer rock formations of the Midland Valley of Scotland.

From time to time, in our geological past, molten lava has been forced towards the Earth's surface. This could erupt from volcanoes, but more frequently cooled and solidified within the upper crust, forming long igneous intrusions known as dykes and sills. Often, lumps of the bedrock would be broken and carried away by the sheer force of the volcanic activity. The same thing could happen to already solidified lava. The alien rocks formed are known as xenoliths.

By studying xenoliths, looking closely at the degree of change they have undergone, scientists have been able to unlock many secrets of our geological past.

Xylomancy

Xylomancy is the ancient art of divination using twigs and rods of wood. Xylomancy is derived from Greek *xulon* – wood – and *mantis* – a prophet or seer. Even today xylomancy is practiced by many people, often quite unaware of the Greek word. 'Dowsing' is usually carried out with a forked twig, which is activated by underground water. And no conjurer would be without a magic wand!

Helen Duncan, born in Callander in 1897, was a famous witch of her day and known to be skilled in xylomancy. She was also the last person to be convicted under the 1735 Witchcraft Act, sentenced to nine months with no right of appeal. The case was brought early in 1944, to keep her under wraps during the planning stages for D-Day. Her powers caused considerable concern at the highest level.

In 1941 this witch had revealed the loss of HMS *Barham*, at the cost of 861 lives, torpedoed by U-boat U331. At the time this was Top Secret information, known only to a few people. No wonder Duncan had the authorities worried. Kept under constant surveillance and subjected to numerous investigations, no fraud or misrepresentation was ever proved against the Callander Witch.

Man has had a long affinity with wood and trees. The name 'druid' comes from the Gaelic *dhariach*, meaning oak, and every letter of the Celtic alphabet is associated with a tree. Rowans are grown for protection and should never be felled. Hazel, second only in power to the rowan, is widely used to provide shanks for walking sticks and shepherds' crooks, and rods for water diviners.

Y

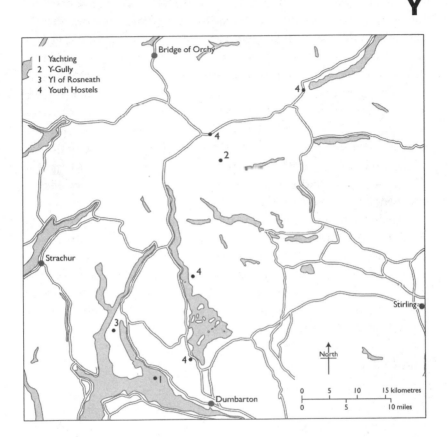

1 Yachting
2 Y-Gully
3 YI of Rosneath
4 Youth Hostels

Yachting

The imposition of duty, to be paid on both imports and exports, has long been a bone of contention. On one side of the Atlantic it led to direct action, the infamous Boston Tea Party, and all that followed. Elsewhere the solution was somewhat more circumspect. Around the coast of Ireland and along the western seaboard of Scotland, small, fast, manoeuvrable and, above all, quiet boats were developed to carry contraband – yachts. The word yacht comes from the Dutch *jagen* – to chase – and schip – a ship. So, *jahtschip* or *jaghte* is a yacht.

Throughout the 18th and early 19th centuries, a great deal of smuggling was conducted under sail, mostly by simply outrunning the authorities. In such activities the men of the Clyde were well and truly in the van, and they were reputed to be the most elusive. Every loss to the Exchequer was someone else's gain.

In 1824 the Irish and Scottish yachtsmen came together to form the Northern Yacht Club. After just three years they went their separate ways, not rejoining again until becoming the Royal Northern and Clyde Yacht Club in 1978. The Royal epithet was bestowed upon the Clyde YC in 1872. With a grand headquarters at Rhu, the Royal Northern and Clyde is one of a number of yacht clubs on the estuary.

Yachting is by no means confined to the sea. Many of our lochs have sailing clubs, some with an equally illustrious history. The Loch Lomond Sailing Club, now based at Millarochy, started with a clubhouse at Rosneath in 1873 – for canoes. Those early pioneers thought nothing about paddling to the Outer Hebrides. Even a small club like Loch Ard can boast a current double Olympic Gold Medallist. Roll on the 2008 Games.

Yggdrasill

What must be the oldest story to tell is that of the creation of the first human, formed from the one living thing to link earth, heaven and hell – Yggdrasill, the great ash tree. The roots, trunk and branches bound the three elements at a time when there were no people on earth, only animals. Many attempts had been made to populate the world, with varying degrees of success. Strange and misshapen creatures had appeared, but no men.

The ancient gods frequently vied with each other to see who could create the perfect being. Then, one day, all the gods took up the challenge at the same time. The power of heaven clashed with the might of the underworld, and the whole world shook from top to bottom. A thunderbolt tore a limb from the ash, sending the shattered wood to the ground below. Swallowed by a deep pool, frozen solid by the night and then thawed by the day, the splintered wood rose up, fashioned into the first of mankind.

This is a story found in distant theology right across northern Europe. *Yggr* means frightful, and was one of the names of the Norse god Odin. *Drasill* is a very old and obscure word for a horse. Odin was believed to have hanged himself from Yggdrasill, so that he would be carried to a place of greater enlightenment. Oak crafted Viking longboats had their magical parts carved from ash – a superstition continued by sailors today.

The Celts also held great store by the ash, believing it to be as potent as mandrake. It can produce beneficial remedies for the treatment of fevers, rheumatism and liver diseases. The midwinter Yule log came from the ash tree, as did the summertime Maypole. And St Patrick chased the snakes from the Emerald Isle with an ash stick.

Y-Gully

For mountaineers, the Y-gully of Cruach Ardrain is sumptuously inviting at any time of year, but winter is best. When the ground has been frozen solid and there is a good covering of snow, the Y-gully provides one of the best winter routes to be found. The gully cleaves the mountains on either side, then rises precipitously towards the 3,431 ft/1,046 m summit. Plumes of spindrift often billow from the pointed peak, like a miniature Everest.

Cruach Ardrain is pronounced *Kroo-ach Ar-dran* and means 'the Stack of the High Peak'. Sometimes the translation is given as 'Big Heap', which is rather an injustice. This is a mountain of enormous character, beautifully proportioned and recognisable from afar. She more than holds her own against Ben More and Stobinian, both near neighbours. Cruach Ardrain is one of many Munros around Crianlarich.

The usual approach to the Y-gully is from Crianlarich, accessible by bus and train. A little to the south of the village, on the A82, a footbridge crosses the West Highland Railway. From this point, a path fights its way through one of the ubiquitous conifer plantations besetting our landscape. Once clear of the trees, the summit of the Grey Height and the first leg of the Y, along Meall Dhamh, is at hand. This ridge leads south east to the cruach.

Cruach Ardrain forms the fulcrum of the Y. The right hand spur runs due north, over Stob Garbh and on to Stob Coire Bhuidhe. Below, the gully of Coire Ardrain slopes away towards Crianlarich before disappearing into the forest. The tail of this Y feature points south to Beinn Tulaichean and an alternative approach from Inverlochlarig, in Balquhidder. Whichever route you take, be adequately dressed and correctly prepared.

Yl of Rosneath

Yl is an archaic spelling of isle or island found in this area, especially around Loch Lomond. Yl nam Bock has become Bucinch, 'the Island of the Billy Goat'. Also on the loch are found Yl Aber, Yl Vealach, Yl na Moin, Yl an Castel and Yl Vow – ancient names that are testament to the history of the National Park and surrounding country. In each case the Gaelic *eilean* has simply been contracted to *yl*.

Yl of Rosneath is a peninsula; a Latin word meaning 'almost an island', a very apt description of this finger of land pointing south into the Clyde estuary. With the rugged Highlands and wild clans to the north, the people on the peninsula would indeed have been isolated. Not until the Duke of Argyll completed his road from Arrochar to his residence at Rosneath Castle in 1787 was there a route overland. Most of the communities of Rosneath continued to depend on their ferry services for many more years.

The backbone of Yl of Rosneath courts the 650 ft/200 m contour. The structure is predominantly grey mica schist interspersed with white quartz veins. The greatly warped and folded rock has been turned upside down by the collision of two land masses, coming together between 400 and 600 million years ago. At the southern tip of the peninsula, the schists meet the younger sandstone formations of the Central Belt. This is the western extremity of the Highland Boundary Fault, characterised by outcrops of conglomerate.

Recorded as the Yl of Rosneath in many old documents, and referred to as an island by Sir Walter Scott, the peninsula is a magical place. Inhabited from earliest times, upon the Yl are to be found abundant archaeology, fantastic wildlife and wonderful seascapes.

Youth Hostels

In 2005 the Youth Hostel Association reached a remarkable milestone – 75 years of providing budget accommodation throughout the land. The Scottish Youth Hostel Association came into being in 1931 and now maintains a network of more than 70 hostels across the country. There are four hostels within the Loch Lomond and Trossachs National Park – Killin, Rowardennan, Arden (Loch Lomond) and Crianlarich.

But the first hostel in the area, established at Ledard Farm, Kinlochard, predates anything the Youth Hostel Association has to offer. This was built by a band of young Glaswegians, in a bid to escape the grime of Clydeside industry. With everything packed into backpacks ready for their Friday evening hooters, they were known as the Rucksack Club. The club eventually merged with the SYHA, later moving into much larger premises overlooking Loch Ard. Like many others, the Kinlochard hostel has been closed and sold off, ending a truly important link with the past.

There are public transport services to all four Scottish Youth Hostels in the area. The magnificent, baronial style hostel at Arden is accessible by bus and train – Balloch is the nearest station. On the other side of Loch Lomond, Rowardennan can only be reached by the ferry from Luss – and then only during the summer months. Crianlarich is served by bus and train and, like the hostel at Rowardennan, is an important staging post on the West Highland

Way. The Killin Hostel provides similar facilities on the Rob Roy Way, almost halfway between Drymen and Pitlochry. There are good bus services, including the postbus, to and from Killin.

Z

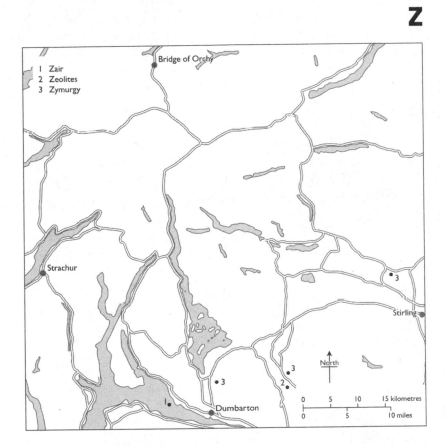

1 Zair
2 Zeolites
3 Zymurgy

Zair

After Caxton had invented his press and printing replaced the hand drawn letter, the Scots lost a letter of their own alphabet. This would have been pronounced as *yogh* and written like a lower case 'z', only with a longer tail. As there was no glyph in an English printing set for this Scottish sound, the letter 'z' was used instead. This accounts for 'z' being used for the 'y' sound in many Scottish words and names, such as capercailzie and Dalziel... and zair.

Zair is also in the dictionary as 'yair', after the way in which the word is spoken. A zair is a well constructed fish trap which seems to be unique to the waters of the Clyde and the Gare Loch. Simple, robust and extremely efficient, it is a wonder that zairs are so localised. There are several good examples of old fish zairs either side of Ardmore Point, between Helensburgh and Dumbarton.

A zair is built on a beach, between the high and low water marks. A wall of boulder and stone is put up around three sides of a rectangle, leaving the side facing the shore open. Twice every day the tide flows in, bringing the fish with it. On the ebb tide, some of the fish are trapped inside the zair and left to await collection – simple, easy and perfectly safe.

Zairs are going the same way as poor old *yogh*; still around but not much use. That's what they call progress. Zair, at least, adheres to its original pronunciation – the yogh sound has not always fared so well and the 'z' has often taken over its role. When pronouncing the name Menzies, for example, some people say MenZies, others say Ming-es – a sort of halfway compromise. With the name Mackenzie, no matter how it is spelled, the 'z' has been fully adopted. That's life. Given time, everything changes.

Zeolites

Zeolites form a group of glassy minerals composed of hydrated aluminium silicates of calcium, sodium or potassium. Crystals of zeolite are formed where mineral rich water gets into fissures and cavities within cooling lava. The word is taken from Greek *zein* – to boil – and *lithos* – stone.

In 1856, work started on the Loch Katrine water scheme, aiming to provide Glasgow with a clean water supply. At Milngavie, a team of 5,000 men laboured to build holding reservoirs to collect the water, and began digging a trench towards the Highlands. The very first section, between Mugdock and Strathblane, threw up large amounts of zeolites amongst the spoil. Rock collectors descended like locusts.

An orange, translucent, coffin shaped crystal known as Heulandite was one of several zeolites to be found. Another was Stilbite, formed into sheaf-like shapes of vitreous, blood orange crystals. The more opaque, pearly white Thomsonite is also sometimes flushed or lined with orange. With many other minerals to search for, this length of the aqueduct was a geologist's paradise.

A second squad of 7,000 workers started at the head of Strathard, digging southwards and tunnelling north through Meall Meadhonach to let out the water. The tunnel is 6,975 ft/2,126 m long. In the first month, mining around the clock, they had excavated 31 inches/79 cm into the hill. The 26-mile project took only forty months to complete, at a cost of £700,000. Those were the days.

Zodiac

Zodiac comes from the Greek word *zoidiakos* – signs. The zodiac is the belt across the night sky through which the moon and planets appear to move. It contains the 12 zodiacal constellations essential to astrology. The signs of our zodiac are Roman in origin; the Greeks and Arabs saw different images shining through the darkness, while the Celts told their own stories around the ceilidh fires.

To the Celts, the most important part of the sky was the zenith, the point right overhead, which they always feared would fall on their heads. The zenith is where we find the constellation called the Plough. The Americans know the same group of stars as the Big Dipper. But our ancestors saw a different image in these stars and, seeing them, would recount one of the great adventures of Finn McCoul.

Finn and his people only had two interests in life, fighting and hunting. There once came a long time of peace, so a splendid stag hunt was arranged. The hunt went right around the world. It went around the world a second time. Soon only two magnificent stags were left alive. The gods took pity on these noble beasts and spirited them away to celestial safety. It was only after dark that Finn realised where his quarry had gone. He decided to build a stairway to the heavens, to finish off the stags. He fired a flaming arrow, which affixed itself to the firmament. A series of fire arrows quickly formed a link to the sky, each one embedded in the shaft of another.

Then word of an impending battle drew Finn away, but not before he had sent five of his best hunting dogs to keep track of his prey. The five hounds, and a wee pup smuggled up in his grandfather's shaggy coat, endlessly pursue the two majestic stags – forever aligned in perfect hunting formation.

Zubenubi

Zubenubi is the shortened form of Zubenelgenubi, the 39th star of navigation. With the importance of sailing in this part of the world, Zubenubi would have been a valuable point of reference during the hours of darkness. The name comes from Arabic, meaning the Southern Claw (of Scorpio). The Greeks also recognised the constellation of the scorpion, seeing it as slayer of the great hunter, Orion.

The Romans, of course, took a different view. From the time of Julius Caesar, in the first century BC, they saw this star as belonging to Libra, the scales – the only inanimate sign of the zodiac. The scales are held aloft by Themis, the goddess of justice, in the guise of the neighbouring figure of Virgo. Themis became the second wife of Zeus and gave mankind the Oracle, the rules of human behaviour.

Zubenelgenubi is an interesting star in a rather faint constellation, through which the low sun passes during the month of November. Seventy-seven light years away, this is actually a double star, comprising a blue-white magnitude 2.7 and a close white magnitude 5.2. In ancient times Arabs used double stars as a test for eyesight. Only the sharpest of eyes will be able to distinguish stars closer than three minutes of arc. As a guide, the moon has 30 minutes of arc.

Modern technology and navigational aids have replaced the need for clear skies to fix a position. However, it is still well worth gazing up into the night sky. Watch out for zodiacal light, scattered by particles of meteoritic debris sinking towards the sun. The best viewing times are spring mornings and autumn evenings – but, for best results, the sky must be quite black.

Zygaena

Zygaena is a genus of distinctive day-flying moth. Our main species is *filipendulae*, better known as the 6-spot Burnet Moth. *Burnet* derives from Old French, meaning dark, which also gives us the word 'brunette'. This moth has butterfly-like clubbed antennae and a wingspan of little more than an inch (28–35 mm). The deep blue-green metallic colour has six crimson spots splashed onto the forewings, giving the moth its common name.

A conspicuous day-flying moth is bound to attract attention – and not just from admirers. Predators are actually warned off by the bright colouration. An extra flash of the red hind wings, fringed in black, reinforces the fact that this moth is very distasteful. Burnet moths can exude droplets of cyanides that are toxic to warm-blooded enemies. For this reason, predatory birds and animals give *Zygaena* species a wide berth.

The 6-spot Burnet Moth is very common on permanent pasture and meadowland during the high summer – July and August. On sunny days, roadside verges can be alive with these moths as they flit from grass to grass. The caterpillars are short and plump, pale yellow in colour, splodged with black. Small bristles give them added protection. The bright yellow bird's foot trefoil provides the food for this stage of their lifecycle.

The tough, yellow cocoons will be fixed high on grass stalks. Surprisingly, the caterpillar re-emerges! Only then will it shed its final pupal skin, which is left hanging from the empty cocoon, and a new moth takes to the wing. In and around the Loch Lomond and Trossachs National Park there are many areas of undisturbed, well-drained, mowed or grazed grassland where *Zygaena* moths can flourish.

Zymurgy

Zymo is Greek, indicating fermentation, as in *zymology*. Zymurgy is the specialised branch of chemistry concerned with the process of fermentation and distilling. Three thousand years ago, the ancient Greeks discovered the secrets of using yeast to turn simple, sweet, fruity liquids into something much more interesting. Fruit was converted into wine, and cereals fermented into ale – party time had really arrived!

The Arabs were first to coin the word alcohol, as *al-kuhl*. You would not want to drink it though. *Al-kuhl* was a very fine powder used to colour the eyebrows black. Our alcohol is quite different, formed by yeast as it turns a sugary solution into energy and carbon dioxide. The alcohol soon begins to kill off the yeast, leaving only a rather weak wine or beer. This is where the process of distillation comes into the story.

The Arabs certainly knew about distillation, but only used it to produce exotic perfumes – not much good for drinking. It was the Celts who perfected the skills of selectively removing and concentrating the alcohol from a weaker solution. You can just imagine a group of our forefathers, sheltering in a cave on a cold winter's night, mulling their ale, suddenly realising that the clear liquid condensing on the stone ceiling is a good deal more palatable than what's in their cups.

The Gaelic *uisge beatha* – water of life – has given us the word whisky. Only five simple and quite natural ingredients are required, all equally important. The malted barley (germinated) and pure water are given added piquancy from the peat. The clear, distilled spirit is aged in fine oak casks and surrounded by the atmosphere which, through the passage of time, will bring the finest of malt whisky to full maturation.

NOTES

NOTES

NOTES

NOTES

NOTES

Some other books published by **LUATH** PRESS

Red Sky at Night
John Barrington
ISBN: 0 946487 60 X PBK £8.99

This fascinating insight into a shepherd's life took *Red Sky at Night* to the top of the UK bestsellers charts on first publication. Now with this new Luath edition a new generation of readers can discover the rhythms of the seasons, spend the night on the hill and learn the mysteries of how shepherds communicate with their dogs. From the reviews the book has received, it might be that the old chant, red sky at night, shepherd's delight, could be reworked: Red Sky at Night, reader's delight!

Mr Barrington is a great pleasure to read.
One learns more things about the countryside
from this account of one year than from a
decade of The Archers.

THE DAILY TELEGRAPH

Powerful and evocative... a book which brings
vividly to life the landscape, the wildlife,
the farm animals and the people who inhabit
John's vista. He makes it easy for the reader to
fall in love with both his surrounds and his
commune with nature.

THE SCOTTISH FIELD

An excellent and informative book... not only an
account of a shepherd's year but also the diary
of a naturalist. Little escapes Barrington's
enquiring eye and, besides the life cycle of
a sheep, he also gives those of every bird,
beast, insect and plant that crosses his path,
mixing their histories with descriptions of
the geography, local history and folklore of
his surroundings.

TLS

The family life at Glengyle is wholesome,
appealing and not without a touch of the Good
Life. Many will envy Mr Barrington his fastness
home as they cruise up Loch Katrine on the
tourist steamer.

THE FIELD

The Underground City, a novel set in Scotland
Jules Verne
ISBN: 1 84282 080 X PBK £7.99

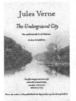

Ten years after he left the exhausted Aberfoyle mine underneath Loch Katrine, the former manger – James Starr – receives an intriguing letter from the old overman – Simon Ford. It suggests that the mine isn't actually barren after all. Despite also receiving an anonymous letter the same day contradicting this, James returns to Aberfoyle and discovers that there is indeed more coal left in the mine to be excavated. However, they are beset by strange events, hinting at a presence that does not wish to see them mine the cave further. Firstly, a stone is thrown at James, but there doesn't seem to have been anyone there. Then, the leaking gas proving that the new mine exists is covered up, and finally James, Simon, and his family are trapped within the new mine as someone, or something, mysteriously blocks up the entrance which they had blown open.

Could it be a person out to sabotage their work? Someone with a grudge against them? Or could it be something supernatural, something they cannot see or understand?

This is a new translation of Jules Verne's novel set underneath Loch Katrine.

Verne is delighting in these details, the science,
mythology and geography of the place. Most of
Verne's books went through some kind of
treatment: some were seen as anti-English,
and these parts were taken out, while sometimes
one third disappeared.

SUNDAY HERALD

One of the strangest and most beautiful novels
of the 19th century.

MICHEL TOURNIER

Luath Press Limited

committed to publishing well written books worth reading

LUATH PRESS takes its name from Robert Burns, whose little collie Luath (*Gael.*, swift or nimble) tripped up Jean Armour at a wedding and gave him the chance to speak to the woman who was to be his wife and the abiding love of his life. Burns called one of The Twa Dogs' Luath after Cuchullin's hunting dog in *Ossian's Fingal*. Luath Press was established in 1981 in the heart of Burns country, and is now based a few steps up the road from Burns' first lodgings on Edinburgh's Royal Mile.

Luath offers you distinctive writing with a hint of unexpected pleasures.

Most bookshops in the UK, the US, Canada, Australia, New Zealand and parts of Europe either carry our books in stock or can order them for you. To order direct from us, please send a £sterling cheque, postal order, international money order or your credit card details (number, address of cardholder and expiry date) to us at the address below. Please add post and packing as follows: UK – £1.00 per delivery address; overseas surface mail – £2.50 per delivery address; overseas airmail – £3.50 for the first book to each delivery address, plus £1.00 for each additional book by airmail to the same address. If your order is a gift, we will happily enclose your card or message at no extra charge.

Luath Press Limited
543/2 Castlehill
The Royal Mile
Edinburgh EH1 2ND
Scotland
Telephone: 0131 225 4326 (24 hours)
Fax: 0131 225 4324
email: sales@luath.co.uk
Website: www.luath.co.uk